# THE POWER OF SUFFERING

## MacArthur Study Series Titles

*Anxiety Attacked*

*Different by Design*

*First Love*

*God: Coming Face to Face with His Majesty*

*How to Meet the Enemy*

*The Power of Suffering*

*Saved without a Doubt*

# THE POWER OF SUFFERING

*Strengthening
Your Faith
in the
Refiner's Fire*

# John MacArthur, Jr.

**VICTOR BOOKS**

A DIVISION OF SCRIPTURE PRESS PUBLICATIONS INC.
USA CANADA ENGLAND

Editor: Barbara Williams
Designer: Andrea Boven
ISBN: 1-56476-429-X

1   2   3   4   5   6   7   8   9   10   Printing/Year   99   98   97   96   95

# CONTENTS

Introduction                                        7

1.  Suffering in the Plan of God                   15

2.  Examples of Faith in the Fire                  43

3.  Paul: A Profile in Suffering                   65

4.  The Silence of the Lamb of God                 91

5.  Preparing for Suffering                       103

6.  Dealing with Suffering                        119

7.  The Lessons from Suffering                    135

    Personal and Group Study Guide               153

    Scripture Index                              175

    Subject Index                                183

# INTRODUCTION

The atmosphere surrounding today's evangelical church, with its emphasis on easy believism and "feel-good-about-yourself" Christianity, has fostered an unbiblical attitude among believers toward the existence of suffering and persecution in their lives. In addition to the natural aversion to pain and difficulty, many Christians have acquired the notion that hardships should not even cross their paths. When various difficulties do come their way, they believe these difficulties are not from God. But this has not been the mind-set of Christians from the earliest days of the church.

An important example of how Christians in other eras dealt with persecution is the case of Martin Luther, the great Reformation leader of the sixteenth century. Even before the debates and controversies of the Reformation were fully underway, Luther was known for his faithfulness to the truth: "The firmness with which Luther relied on the Holy Scriptures imparted great authority to his teaching. But other circumstances added still more to his strength. In him every action of his life corresponded with his words. It was known that these discourses did not proceed merely from his lips: they had their source in his heart, and were practiced in all his works" (J.H. Merle D'Aubigne, *The Life and Times of Martin Luther* [Chicago: Moody, 1978], 67).

Luther's most well-known stand for truth happened in the spring of 1521. By then he had already been excommunicated from the Roman Church and was known throughout most of Europe as the leading critic of the church. Luther earnestly and persistently taught justification by faith alone and the supremacy of the Scripture's authority. The church opposed Luther on these and other points and vigorously tried to silence him. He was ordered to appear before an assembly (Diet of Worms) of secular and church leaders in Germany to explain his teachings. The assembly hoped Luther, under the intense pressure and intimidation of being "called on the carpet," would retract his views and give the church and empire some peace.

But Luther stood firm for his convictions. When the leaders of the assembly at Worms insisted that he retract all his past statements, Luther refused:

> Unless therefore I am convinced by the testimony of Scripture, or by the clearest reasoning — unless I am persuaded by means of the passages I have quoted — and unless they thus render my conscience bound by the Word of God, I cannot and I will not retract, for it is unsafe for a Christian to speak against his conscience. . . . Here I stand, I can do no other; May God help me! Amen! (quoted in D'Aubigne, 433)

Luther's handling of this personal crisis and challenge testified to the greatness and sufficiency of God.
At such a tension-filled, pivotal juncture in the Reformer's life, his reactions to the events must have been
pleasing to the Lord. Luther did not react with anger or
second-guess God for his difficulties. Neither did he
turn away from the situation in cowardly fear. Instead,
Luther lived out Jesus' promises in Matthew 10:18-20,
"And you shall even be brought before governors and
kings for My sake, as a testimony to them and to the
Gentiles. But when they deliver you up, do not become
anxious about how or what you will speak; for it shall
be given you in that hour what you are to speak. For it
is not you who speak, but it is the Spirit of your Father
who speaks in you."

Christians at the end of the twentieth century are
unlikely to face the kind of opposition Martin Luther
did during the early part of the sixteenth century. It is
also unlikely that most believers will ever face the imminent threat of martyrdom. However, I believe it is
more difficult to make such assertions with certainty
today than it was thirty or forty years ago. Conditions
within our post-Christian culture and an unstable evangelical church are changing and declining so rapidly
that believers need to be prepared and not get caught
off guard when confronted with persecutions and various hardships. Job 5:7 speaks of humanity's general
condition and what we ought to expect: "For man is
born for trouble, as sparks fly upward." Concerning the
potential persecution of believers, the Apostle Paul is
even more pointed: "And indeed, all who desire to live
godly in Christ Jesus will be persecuted" (2 Tim. 3:12).

"Christian bashing" is increasingly popular. It has
become a favorite pastime among journalists in the lib-

eral media and among liberals in education, the arts, and politics. Bigotry is back in style, and the politically correct form of it is to assault Christians. Often it is those who preach "tolerance," "nonjudgmentalism," and "intellectualism" who are most intolerant.

A recent issue of the *National and International Religion Report* (February 6, 1995, p. 5) reported that seventeen Christians have been arrested in Nepal since September 1994, mostly for evangelizing. Eleven will be tried and could get three years in prison if convicted.

According to David Barrett, editor of *World Christian Encyclopedia*, 300,000 Christians are martyred each year—833 per day. Barrett concludes that the worldwide chance of being a martyr as a Christian is 1 in 200. If you are a missionary, 1 in 50. If you are a native evangelist, 1 in 20 (New York: Oxford University Press, 1982).

Certainly with the increase in godless secularism and as we near the return of Christ, we could expect that such hostility and persecution might grow.

With its many allurements, Satan uses the world system constantly to entice and wear down true Christians everywhere. The challenge of worldly attractions is, I believe, even more difficult for American believers. Our culture's subtle persecutions often lead to individual and group compromise, offering just enough acceptance of Christians and the church generally to sway unsuspecting believers. Before long they become apathetic and afraid to make Christianity an issue. In such an environment it becomes increasingly difficult to maintain an untainted Christian testimony. By contrast, in totalitarian societies where a high cost is associated with Christianity, it might just be easier to sustain a consistent testimony.

For example, I remember once asking a Russian

pastor if it was difficult to pastor a local church when the society and government were so hostile to Christianity. He answered, "It's easy. You always know where everyone stands. What I don't understand is how in the world you can pastor a church in America where the compromises are so common and subtle."

If there are confusing thoughts and misplaced expectations among believers concerning persecutions, there is also much misunderstanding concerning the more general role of trials, sufferings, and troubles in the Christian life. We tend to forget even the basic fact that all people live in a fallen world—we are sinful creatures living in a corrupt, sin-cursed society. Believers should not be surprised, perplexed, or resentful when they encounter difficulties throughout this life.

Job 14:1 says, "Man, who is born of woman, is short-lived and full of turmoil." In Psalm 22:11 David said, "Be not far from me, for trouble is near." The Preacher in the Book of Ecclesiastes summarized well life's difficulty when he wrote, "So I hated life, for the work which had been done under the sun was grievous to me; because everything is futility and striving after wind" (2:17).

Jesus tells us we should expect troubles: "In the world you have tribulation" (John 16:33). He Himself did not avoid dealing with hardships and experiencing feelings of distress: "When Jesus therefore saw her weeping, and the Jews who came with her, also weeping, He was deeply moved in spirit, and was troubled" (11:33; see also Mark 14:33).

In 2 Corinthians 4:8-9 the Apostle Paul, based on personal experience, gives a partial list of his troubles: "We are afflicted in every way, but not crushed; perplexed, but not despairing; persecuted, but not forsaken; struck down, but not destroyed." Even history's greatest evangelist and missionary was not immune to sufferings, trials, and persecutions.

So we see that in God's sovereignty all kinds of difficulties and hardships are real and should be expected in the lives of genuine Christians. One primary reason many believers today have a hard time accepting the role of suffering in their lives or in the lives of friends and loved ones is that they have failed to understand and accept the reality of divine sovereignty. Many also fail to see adversity from God's perspective. In so doing, they completely overlook the positive, strengthening, perfecting effect that trials are designed to have on believers' faith. In chapter 1 we will examine in more detail the reasons for suffering and look at some of God's purposes behind trials and persecutions.

In chapters 2–4 we'll look at the lives of several people in the Bible who dealt with and endured suffering in extraordinarily godly ways. We'll begin in chapter 2 with three case studies: Stephen, the first martyr of the church; Daniel's three friends in the fiery furnace; and Daniel in the lions' den.

In chapter 3 we'll continue our character studies with a view of the Apostle Paul's persecution-filled ministry. From the beginning of his service for Christ, Paul had the right perspective on suffering and was a role model for believers (Phil. 3:7-11).

Our study of role models will culminate in chapter 4 with a consideration of how our ultimate example, the Lord Jesus, dealt with suffering. As this chapter unfolds it will become clear that the key to being like Christ in the midst of suffering and persecution is to be like Him at all other times.

The final three chapters constitute the heart of the

book. In these chapters it is my sincere hope that we can draw together our examination of the power of suffering with some practical applications and exhortations. The real key in accepting and enduring a particular trial or persecution, or in persevering victoriously through a certain period of suffering, is discipleship. In chapters 5 and 6 you will see that believers need not live in fear of suffering or be caught completely off guard when it comes. A realistic expectancy, coupled with solid spiritual preparedness derived from the truth of God's Word, is more than sufficient for us as we confront any crisis.

The conclusion of any scriptural study of believers and suffering is this: it is possible, and actually God's desire, that we do more than merely survive or barely tolerate a season of testing or suffering. The Lord wants the experience, though perhaps difficult as we pass through it, to be a positive one in the end—one that strengthens and refines our faith (Job 23:10). In chapter 7 we'll focus on that truth.

As you read this book it is my earnest hope that you will receive fresh new insights into the role of suffering in the Christian life. I pray that whatever misconceptions or doubts you have about the place of suffering in God's plan will fade away. May you instead, by His grace, be conformed ever more to the image of Christ as you understand better the refining power that pain and adversity exercise in the believer's life.

# ONE

# Suffering in the Plan of God

The average person who follows the news at all is aware of the constant barrage of negative stories, tragic reports of death, disaster, and violence, and a whole variety of simply puzzling items that to differing degrees defy explanation. During 1994 several major accidents happened, including an airliner crash near Pittsburgh and a ferry boat capsizing in the Baltic Sea. People were almost compulsive in seeking reasons for the incidents. It is natural to want to know the direct earthly causes and motivations that lead to sad, troubling, or tragic occurrences. On the other hand, most people shy away from looking beyond the temporal to find spiritual answers to life's more difficult events.

Biblically literate Christians, however, will realize that God's sovereignty has a role in all events—from the most pleasant and easiest to accept to the most traumatic and hardest to understand. But even the most mature believer can at times struggle to accept or even perceive God's purposes for adversity. Those who don't recognize the Lord's sovereign role will tend to question why troubles are happening to them at all.

The writers of the older hymns usually had a proper perspective on adversity. Consider, for example, the marvelous words of Samuel Rodigast from the first stanza of the seventeenth-century hymn, "What'er My God Ordains Is Right."

> Whate'er my God ordains is right: holy His will abideth;
> I will be still whate'er He doth, and follow where He guideth:
> He is my God; though dark my road, He holds me that I shall not fall:
> wherefore to Him I leave it all.

We can rest assured that even if we do not see or understand the reason for a particular instance of adversity and are caught off guard, God is not. Jesus, as God's Son, knew that trials and persecutions were to be expected within the experiences of all genuine believers through the centuries.

## JESUS PREDICTS HOSTILITY FROM THE WORLD

In the midst of His Upper Room Discourse Jesus warned the disciples that "If the world hates you, you know that it has hated Me before it hated you. If you were of the world, the world would love its own; but because you are not of the world, but I chose you out of the world, therefore the world hates you" (John 15:18-19). This statement simply reinforced what He said earlier in His ministry during the Sermon on the Mount:

> Blessed are those who have been persecuted for the sake of righteousness, for theirs is the kingdom of heaven. Blessed are you when men revile you, and persecute you, and say all kinds of evil against you falsely, on account of Me. Rejoice, and be glad, for your reward in heaven is great, for so they persecuted the prophets who were before you (Matt. 5:10-12).

It is clear from these and other warnings (see Mark 13:9-13) that Jesus saw animosity toward believers from the unbelieving world, along with whatever pain and suffering that might accompany it, as normal and expected.

## WHY DOES THE WORLD HATE US?

Two violent events, occurring just forty-eight hours apart, stunned the nation during the last weekend of February 1993. First, six people were killed and a thousand injured in New York City when a powerful bomb exploded beneath the twin skyscrapers of the World Trade Center. (By early May, seven men with ties to Middle Eastern Islamic terrorist groups had been arrested in connection with the bombing.) Then, two days after the bombing, four federal agents were killed during an unsuccessful raid on the Branch Davidian cult compound near Waco, Texas. That led to a fifty-one-day standoff between the government and the religious cult, which ended tragically when the compound burned down, killing at least seventy-five.

Fanaticism and hateful intolerance played a part in both those stories—and they are merely two from among many such examples in recent years. Even a

casual observer of modern society will find incidents of
ethnic bigotry and racial hate crimes in any larger
American city. There is also much animosity and con-
tention between groups with competing social and political viewpoints. But none of those conflicts is as significant as the one between Christians and the world.

### Because We Oppose the World

First, the world hates Christians primarily because
Christians are not of the world. We are not culturally
part of the "in group." We move against the main-
stream secular flow of ideas and practices and stand
opposed to wrongs and injustices. We are even eager to
urge individuals to repent of their sins and turn to
Christ. This final characteristic generates the most intense opposition and hatred from the world.

The term "world" as used in John 15 and elsewhere
is translated from the Greek *kosmos*. In this context it
refers to the evil system of sin in the world, as authored
by Satan and acted out by humanity. In starker terms,
we could say it is the depraved society of wicked human beings that has set itself against Christ, His kingdom, and His people. Is it any wonder that, with Satan
at the head of such a system (see 12:31; 14:30), believers
should face hateful opposition when they confront that
society?

Disguised as an "angel of light" (2 Cor. 11:14), Satan
presents his world system as a false religion. This religion so often presents itself to Christians under the
subtle guise of false godliness, which appears to be
tolerant of God and Christ when in reality it opposes the
truth and openly persecutes believers if necessary. Such
deception often makes Christians think there is no threat
or leads to surprise when outward persecution comes.

It was a religious system that hated Jesus so much that it eventually killed Him. The false religionists of Palestine detested Him because He violated their system and rebuked their hypocrisy with His righteousness. Similarly, Abel in Genesis 4 was killed by false religion personified in his brother Cain. First John 3:12 provides us with commentary on what Cain did: "Not as Cain, who was of the evil one, and slew his brother. And for what reason did he slay him? Because his deeds were evil, and his brother's were righteous."

Because of the nature of Satan's false system over the centuries, with its evil, relentless opposition to God's kingdom, it is important that Christians realize they are not part of the world. God has called us to stand for Jesus Christ in the midst of a sinful society. The system is at once the enemy and the mission field. Paul urged the Philippians to live righteously so "that you may prove yourselves to be blameless and innocent, children of God above reproach in the midst of a crooked and perverse generation, among whom you appear as lights in the world" (Phil. 2:15). This admonition correlates well with what Jesus already said in the Sermon on the Mount: "You are the salt of the earth; but if the salt has become tasteless, how will it be made salty again? It is good for nothing any more, except to be thrown out and trampled under foot by men. You are the light of the world. A city set on a hill cannot be hidden" (Matt. 5:13-14).

Such exhortations call for Christians to be the conscience of a sinful and perverse generation. If we are obedient and take the scriptural injunctions seriously, we should not be surprised by hostility and persecution. Jesus Himself faced harsh opposition from the people of His day even when He rebuked them more indirectly regarding their spiritual attitude (Luke 4:25-30).

### Because It Hates Christ

If the religious leaders hated Jesus so much, can believers today expect things to be easier for them? Jesus answers that in John 15:20, "Remember the word that I said to you, 'A slave is not greater than his master.' If they persecuted Me, they will also persecute you; if they kept My word, they will keep yours also." If as Christians we are in Christ and Christ is in us (Gal. 2:20; Col. 2:10-12), the world will hate us even as it hated Christ.

This second aspect of why the world hates us should actually bring us happiness. If we receive suffering and persecution from the world because we represent Jesus, we experience the fellowship of His sufferings. The disciples in Acts 5:41, after being flogged by the religious authorities for continuing to teach in Jesus' name, displayed this attitude of joy: "So they went on their way from the presence of the Council, rejoicing that they had been considered worthy to suffer shame for His name."

Paul spoke of that fellowship of sufferings in Philippians 3:10 and he knew quite well what that meant (see 2 Cor. 4:7-18). Scripture attests to the fact that Paul lived out what he taught and wrote. (We will deal in more depth later with Paul's marvelous example of facing suffering.)

### Because It Does Not Know God

A third reason the world hates Christians is that it does not know God. In John 15 Jesus says, "But all these things they will do to you for My name's sake, *because they do not know the One who sent Me"* (v. 21, emphasis added). Such ignorance of God has contributed greatly to horrible spiritual and moral degradation, unawareness of truth, and hostility to what is right. In many ways modern society reflects the first-century conditions in which Paul ministered. When he preached in Athens he saw how misplaced the people's religion was: "And Paul stood in the midst of the Areopagus and said, 'Men of Athens, I observe that you are very religious in all respects. For while I was passing through and examining the objects of your worship, I also found an altar with this inscription, "TO AN UNKNOWN GOD." What therefore you worship in ignorance, this I proclaim to you' " (Acts 17:22-23).

Paul uncovered an apathy and ignorance toward the true God and superstition regarding false gods. Without Paul's commentary, we could easily infer that many unbelievers are sincerely moral and religious people, not really affected that much by sin. But such a perception can lead us to downplay opposition from the world or not be aggressive enough in our evangelism. We often do not take Romans 1:18–2:2 seriously in its picture of the world's natural sinfulness and willful rejection of God's revelation. The world system still does not know God, no matter how tolerant or accepting it might seem when it works through false religion. It still hates believers, still opposes us, and therefore, whatever persecution and pain we receive should not catch us off guard.

Many believers act as if they have beaten the problem of hatred from the world, thinking they are friends of the world. But they forget John's warning, "If any one loves the world, the love of the Father is not in him" (1 John 2:15), or James' strong statement, "Therefore whoever wishes to be a friend of the world makes himself an enemy of God" (James 4:4). Satan tempts us subtly to be comfortable in the world, to feel at home within the system, and to make the world around us feel at ease. We seek not to offend anyone, but that is not what Jesus had in mind. Nor was that Paul's approach:

> For since in the wisdom of God the world through its wisdom did not come to know God, God was well-pleased through the foolishness of the message preached to save those who believe. For indeed Jews ask for signs, and Greeks search for wisdom; but we preach Christ crucified, to Jews a stumbling block, and to Gentiles foolishness, but to those who are the called, both Jews and Greeks, Christ the power of God and the wisdom of God. Because the foolishness of God is wiser than men, and the weakness of God is stronger than men (1 Cor. 1:21-25).

## WHY IS SUFFERING PART OF THE PLAN?

So far in this chapter we have seen that suffering, primarily as the result of persecution, is something that true believers may expect to experience. Jesus predicted there would be troubles in this life (John 16:33), and the apostles supported Him in this teaching (2 Tim. 3:12; 1 Peter 4:12). Even if these statements are obediently and faithfully accepted as true—after all, they are in Scripture—the questions of why, how, and on what basis still arise in the minds of Christians.

Those basic questions, which all honest and searching believers are going to have—to one degree or another based on their level of maturity—can be answered under one all-encompassing reality. That reality is the sovereignty of God which, when rightly understood and properly embraced, serves as the foundational lens through which Christians may see all truths in Scripture more clearly. Knowing about God's sovereignty in all things does not mean we will have comprehensive understanding, but it gives us a proper hope in the midst of the more difficult and less clear aspects of His working in our lives (Gen. 18:25; Isa. 55:9).

A complete study of the sovereignty of God is beyond the scope of this book, but a brief discussion will help put the origin and cause of suffering into context. A.W. Pink gives this concise comment: "To say that God is sovereign is to declare that God *is* God" (*The Sovereignty of God*, rev. ed. [Edinburgh: Banner of Truth, 1961], 20). He then expands on how God's sovereignty is executed.

> The sovereignty of the God of Scripture is absolute, irresistible, infinite. When we say that God is sovereign, we affirm His right to govern the universe, which He has made for His own glory, just as He pleases. We affirm that *His right* is the right of the Potter over the clay, viz.: that He may mould that clay into whatsoever form He chooses, fashioning out of *the same lump* one vessel unto honour and another unto dishonour. We affirm that He is under no rule or law outside His own will and nature, *that God is a law unto Himself*, and that He is under no obligation to give an account of His matters to any. Sovereignty characterizes the whole Being

of God. He is sovereign in all His attributes. *He is sovereign in the exercise of His power.* His power is exercised *as* He wills, *when* He wills, *where* He wills. This fact is evidenced on every page of Scripture. For a long season that power appears to be dormant, and then it goes forth with irresistible might. Pharaoh dared to hinder Israel from going forth to worship Jehovah in the wilderness. What happened? God exercised His power, His people were delivered and their cruel taskmasters slain. But a little later, the Amalekites dared to attack these same Israelites in the wilderness, and what happened? Did God put forth His power on this occasion and display His hand as He did at the Red Sea? Were these enemies of His people promptly overthrown and destroyed? No, on the contrary, the Lord swore that He would "have war with Amalek from *generation to generation*" (Ex. 17:16). Again, when Israel entered the land of Canaan, God's power was signally displayed. The city of Jericho barred their progress. What happened? Israel did not draw a bow nor strike a blow: the Lord stretched forth His hand and the walls fell down flat. But the miracle was never repeated! *No other city fell after this manner.* Every other city had to be captured by the sword! (*The Sovereignty of God,* 22–23, author's emphases)

From that analysis we can infer that God's sovereignty is all powerful but not always predictable from the human standpoint. God is free to do or not do as He chooses in any given situation, and He is not in any way obligated to repeat the same action in connection with any subsequent, similar situation. It is in this way that God sovereignly chooses, as part of His plan, to bring suffering into the lives of various Christians, under differing circumstances, with varying results. In Isaiah 45:7, God says He is "the One forming light and creating darkness, causing well-being and creating calamity; I am the Lord who does all these." Because of His sovereign power "God causes all things to work together for good to those who love God, to those who are called according to His purpose" (Rom. 8:28). Again we can see that God's sphere of operation is comprehensive. Therefore, sufferings, trials, persecutions, and all kinds of adversity that may face believers are certainly under His sovereign control and can originate as part of His sovereign plan.

## LESSONS LEARNED FROM SUFFERING

Knowing that any suffering experienced by believers is part of God's overall sovereign plan provides its own comfort. However, as with any aspect of truth in the Christian life, intellectual knowledge is not an exact parallel to experiential knowledge. Until we know how we react in the midst of living out a certain truth, intellectual allegiance counts for nothing (James 1:25-27; 2:14-17). Testing the validity of what believers profess is one of the fundamental reasons God allows suffering (Job 23:10).

One sure way to test the genuineness of a diamond is by means of what jewelers call the water test. An imitation stone never shines as brilliantly as a real one, but the contrast is not always easy to detect just by ordinary viewing. Jewelers know that placing a genuine diamond and an imitation one side by side in water will reveal the differences. The real one continues to sparkle brilliantly underwater, whereas the fake one loses practically all its sparkle.

As an analogy to this illustration, many people who are very confident in the genuineness of their faith find it lacking when they come under the waters of sorrow or adversity. The supposed diamond brilliance of their faith is then shown to be nothing but an imitation. However, put the true child of God under the water of a trial and he will shine as brilliantly as ever. G.K. Chesterton also used the metaphor of water to make the same point: "I believe in getting into hot water. I think it keeps you clean."

### The Lesson of Faith

It seems clear then that the foremost reason God tests us through suffering is to *test the strength of our faith.* One of the classic case studies in Scripture that illustrates this is the account of Abraham's testing in Genesis 22. It was, in my estimation, the severest trial any human being ever faced.

Genesis 22:1-2 says, "Now it came about after these things, that God tested Abraham, and said to him, 'Abraham!' And he said, 'Here I am.' And He said, 'Take now your son, your only son, whom you love, Isaac, and go to the land of Moriah; and offer him there as a burnt offering on one of the mountains of which I will tell you.' "

This command did not fit Abraham's theology at all. I'm sure it prompted a string of questions for God, such as: Why would You call for human sacrifice when You had never asked for such a pagan thing before? (It was the antithesis of everything Abraham knew to be true about God.) Why would You go to such lengths to enable a husband and wife nearing 100 years of age each, who had been childless their entire married lives, to produce a son and then ask for that son to be killed? Why would You promise me that I would be the father of many nations, with people numbering as the sands of the sea and the stars of heaven, and then ask the son of promise to be killed?

The whole idea was absolutely inconceivable. It was a trial that made no sense—not in terms of God's nature, His plan of redemption, His Word, and His or Abraham's love for Isaac. In addition to these factors, this trial was perhaps the severest ever for a human being because God told Abraham *himself* to kill Isaac. It's one thing to watch a loved one die, it's something else to be told to kill that person.

A straightforward reading of Genesis 22:3-8 reveals how Abraham reacted in this crisis:

> So Abraham rose early in the morning and saddled his donkey, and took two of his young men with him and Isaac his son; and he split wood for the burnt offering, and arose and went to the place of which God had told him. On the third day Abraham raised his eyes and saw the place from a distance. And Abraham said to his young men, "Stay here with the donkey, and I and the lad will go yonder; and we will worship and return to you." And Abraham took the wood of the burnt offering and laid it on Isaac his son, and he took in his hand the fire and the knife. So the two of them walked on together. And Isaac spoke to Abraham his father and said,"My father!" And he said, "Here I am, my son." And he said, "Behold, the fire and

the wood, but where is the lamb for the burnt offering?" And Abraham said, "God will provide for Himself the lamb for the burnt offering, my son." So the two of them walked on together.

Abraham revealed amazing faith in this situation. He obeyed God immediately, without question or argument (v. 3). In verses 5 and 8 he expressed the quiet confidence, first of all, that he and Isaac would return and, second, that God would provide a lamb for the burnt offering. Those facts suggest that deep down in his heart Abraham knew God's action was going to be consistent with His character and covenant. Abraham may not have known specifically what that was, but the passage indicates that he had a good idea.

Genesis 22:9-12 is the climactic segment of Abraham's greatest test:

Then they came to the place of which God had told him; and Abraham built the altar there, and arranged the wood, and bound his son Isaac, and laid him on the altar on top of the wood. And Abraham stretched out his hand, and took the knife to slay his son. But the angel of the Lord called to him from heaven, and said, "Abraham, Abraham!" And he said, "Here I am." And he said, "Do not stretch out your hand against the lad, and do nothing to him; for now I know that you fear God, since you have not withheld your son, your only son, from Me."

This brief examination of this crucial episode in the life of Abraham demonstrates how Paul can say, "Even so Abraham believed God, and it was reckoned to him as righteousness. Therefore, be sure that it is those who are of faith that are sons of Abraham" (Gal. 3:6-7). Abraham was prepared to plunge a knife into the chest of his own son. He was submissive, obedient, and willing to worship God at any cost. God accepted Abraham's willingness as evidence of his faith and clothed him with righteousness.

The writer of Hebrews offers commentary on this trial: "By faith Abraham, when he was tested, offered up Isaac; and he who had received the promises was offering up his only begotten son; it was he to whom it was said, 'In Isaac your seed shall be called.' He considered that God is able to raise men even from the dead; from which he also received him back as a type" (Heb. 11:17-19). Abraham was willing to kill his own son because he believed God would keep His promise of a progeny for Isaac, even if the Lord had to raise the dead Isaac, though to our knowledge Abraham had never known of a resurrection.

Such extraordinary obedience in the face of the severest of trials informs us that a believer today can endure the most difficult trials imaginable if he or she wholeheartedly trusts in God. Abraham's test also informs us that God's tests for us might involve people we hold very near and dear, such as sons, daughters, husbands, wives, or close friends. We may have to offer up our own Isaac—give the ones we love most over to the Lord. We may need to let them go God's way, rather than holding on to them so they'll live the way we'd prefer.

We can conclude that the more difficult the obedience, the more excellent it is. Abraham obeyed God in the extremity, and as a result he became the model of faith. Thus anyone who has faith in God and is thereby justified is a child in the spiritual line of Abraham. If we trust God as Abraham did, we can be confident in any test or trial.

The account of Abraham's great testing in the land of Moriah is perhaps the prime example of a faith-revealing trial. But it is certainly not the only Old Testament illustration we could point to. Second Chronicles 32:31 summarizes Hezekiah's testings from the Lord by stating that the purpose was so "He might know what was in his heart." Surely God does not have to test any of us to find out what is in our hearts because He already knows. Rather, He tests us so that *we* might know what is in our hearts. In that sense He assists us in taking a spiritual inventory and self-examination. Whenever God brings us through a severe trial, it will reveal to us either the strength or weakness of our faith, and the faithfulness of God. If by grace we display a strong faith, that ought to encourage us that it's real and that it can become stronger as we continue to see the Lord through trials (see Job 42:1-6).

### The Lesson of Humility
If you were to take a survey of what profession lacked the most humility, the people you talked to would most likely select athletes. Absurd player salaries, pervasive television coverage, and cutthroat business executives who operate teams as just one element of their larger profit-making enterprises, have supplanted the noble sportsmen who possessed integrity and the highest ideals of fairness, team spirit, and sacrifice. We can't imagine many of today's superstars reacting humbly or meekly to major adversity or a career-ending "bad break." Out of such a negative backdrop, let's briefly

consider one positive example of humility from the past.

Lou Gehrig was one of the greatest players in baseball history. His career as a power-hitting first baseman with the New York Yankees ended just prior to World War II. His playing days were cut short in 1939 by the onset of a rare terminal disease of the nerves and muscles, amyotrophic lateral sclerosis (popularly known now as "Lou Gehrig's disease"). Gehrig handled himself well in the midst of suffering and personal disappointment. His exemplary behavior culminated before a crowd of over 60,000 at Yankee Stadium on July 4, 1939, "Lou Gehrig Day." There on the playing field in front of a clutter of microphones that beamed his voice to additional millions of radio listeners, Lou Gehrig concluded his remarks by saying, "Today, I consider myself the luckiest man on the face of the earth." What a statement to make in light of his circumstances! His health steadily declined from that day until his death two years later.

As far as we know, Lou Gehrig was not a believer. Should not a believer whose life and eternity is controlled for good and glory by God react the same way if he were confronted with the same trial? We should if we realize that a second reason God sends trials is *to humble us.* He uses suffering to remind us not to think more confidently of our spiritual strength than we should (Rom. 12:3).

The wonderful testimony of the Apostle Paul in 2 Corinthians 12 provides one of the best Scripture illustrations of this principle: "There was given me a thorn in the flesh, a messenger of Satan to buffet me — to keep me from exalting myself!" (v. 7) Paul was mindful of the supernatural revelations he had been privi-

leged to see, hear, and experience as part of his ministry. He had seen the exalted Jesus on several occasions
after His resurrection and was even received up into
the third heaven. As a result, Paul easily could have
thought more highly of himself than was wise or acceptable to God.

To preserve his humility, God literally struck Paul
with a very painful, chronic problem, "a messenger of
Satan." That tells us that the "thorn in the flesh" was a
person. "Messenger" is *angelos* in Greek, and is sometimes translated "angel." The word is used 188 times in
the New Testament and always refers to a person. In
2 Corinthians 12 it likely referred to a demon-possessed
man leading the assault on Paul at Corinth.

The precise nature of Paul's problem is not as important as the point God was making to him—and us.
When we are blessed in places of spiritual service, God
sometimes deems it necessary to allow Satan's messen-
gers to batter us to keep us humble. Such troubles
remind us that we have no strength in ourselves and
He is the One who enables us to minister. Divine power is released through such weakness. When we are
without strength, we have to rest in His. Thus Paul
said: "He has said to me, 'My grace is sufficient for you,
for power is perfected in weakness.' Most gladly, therefore, I will rather boast about my weaknesses, that the
power of Christ may dwell in me. Therefore I am well
content with weaknesses, with insults, with distresses,
with persecutions, with difficulties, for Christ's sake; for
when I am weak, then I am strong" (2 Cor. 12:9-10).

### The Lesson of Rejecting Materialism

In spite of the various economic fluctuations, down-
sizings, and lower expectations that have occurred in

recent years, we still live in a very materialistic society. Believers in the United States and other industrialized societies have very high standards of living compared to the rest of the world. The familiar conveniences and comforts, not to mention new products and services, lull us into a sense of ease and convince us that we can't live without them. Our daily lives so readily revolve around possessions—cars, computers, furniture, appliances, financial investments. We all are tempted to fall into the trap that Jesus warned against in Matthew 6:24, "No one can serve two masters; for either he will hate the one and love the other, or he will hold to one and despise the other. You cannot serve God and mammon [riches]." Material wealth prevented the rich young man from entering God's kingdom (Mark 10:17-22).

Because materialism can be such a stumbling block for believers, a serious reflection of these matters leads to a third reason for the Lord bringing us trials: *to wean us away from worldly things.* It has been my observation that most mature Christians, as the years pass by, will attribute less and less significance to the temporal things they've accumulated. At one time those things were the most desirable in life, but they gradually lose that status as the believer becomes aware that they cannot solve major problems or alleviate great anxieties.

When God does send certain trials or sufferings into our lives, they will confirm the inadequacy of material things to meet our deepest needs or to provide any true resources for our time of stress and pain. Through this process the Lord will reveal our need to be weaned away from worldly possessions and riches. Or He may even verify what many of us have already observed—that worldly possessions and temporal experiences are less and less important to us as we become closer to Him.

Moses is a marvelous scriptural example of one who accepted the need to be weaned off dependence on earthly props. Hebrews 11:24-26 contains a concise New Testament commentary on what happened to him: "By faith Moses, when he had grown up, refused to be called the son of Pharaoh's daughter; choosing rather to endure ill-treatment with the people of God, than to enjoy the passing pleasures of sin; considering the reproach of Christ greater riches than the treasures of Egypt; for he was looking to the reward."

Moses had been reared for forty years in Pharaoh's household and educated as a prince of Egypt. He had risen to the top within the society of a leading super-power of his day. Nevertheless, he took his eyes off his prestigious earthly position and became involved with the sufferings of his countrymen, the Israelites, who were oppressed as slaves. The Lord in effect made Israel's trial Moses' trial and weaned him off worldly things.

### The Lesson of Eternal Hope

A fourth purpose the Lord has in sending trials is *to call us to a greater realization of our eternal hope*. To state it more simply, trials make us long for heaven. Consider the death of a loved one who was a believer. If that most precious of persons (spouse, child, some other relative or close friend) is called to heaven, and you are open and accepting of God's sovereignty, you will invariably focus your heart and mind on eternal things. You will quickly develop a disengaged, disinterested relationship with this passing world. Romans 8:18-24 beautifully supports this thought:

For I consider that the sufferings of this present time are not worthy to be compared with the glory that is to be revealed to us. For the anxious longing of the creation waits eagerly for the revealing of the sons of God. For the creation was subjected to futility, not of its own will, but because of Him who subjected it, in hope that the creation itself also will be set free from its slavery to corruption into the freedom of the glory of the children of God. For we know that the whole creation groans and suffers the pains of childbirth together until now. And not only this, but also we ourselves, having the first fruits of the Spirit, even we ourselves groan within ourselves, waiting eagerly for our adoption as sons, the redemption of our body. For in hope we have been saved.

The Apostle Paul lends further support to this premise in 2 Corinthians 4:16-18, where he draws upon his own experiences and summarizes the results of his trials:

Therefore we do not lose heart, but though our outer man is decaying, yet our inner man is being renewed day by day. For momentary, light affliction is producing for us an eternal weight of glory far beyond all comparison, while we look not at the things which are seen, but at the things which are not seen; for the things which are seen are temporal, but the things which are not seen are eternal.

In 2 Corinthians 5:1-8, Paul adds:

We know that if the earthly tent which is our house is torn down, we have a building from God, a house not made with hands, eternal in the heavens. For indeed in this house we groan, longing to be clothed with our dwelling from heaven; inasmuch as we, having put it on, shall not be found naked. For indeed while we are in this tent, we groan, being burdened, because we do not want to be unclothed, but to be clothed, in order that what is mortal may be swallowed up by life. Now He who prepared us for this very purpose is God, who gave to us the Spirit as a pledge. Therefore, being always of good courage, and knowing that while we are at home in the body we are absent from the Lord—for we walk by faith, not by sight—we are of good courage, I say, and prefer rather to be absent from the body and to be at home with the Lord.

Even apart from the context of trials and sufferings, Paul exhorts us to set our minds "on the things above" (Col. 3:1-2).

### The Lesson of First Love

God also uses trials and sufferings for the very important purpose of *showing us what we really love*. That was part of the Lord's test for Abraham at Moriah. The big question Abraham had to answer was *Do you love your son Isaac more than God or do you love God more than Isaac?* In that situation the answer was crucial because God was prepared to remove Isaac from Abraham if that would have given God first place in Abraham's life.

The Lord also tests us to show us the object of our

first love (Deut. 13:3; see also 6:5; Matt. 22:36-37). Jesus brings this matter of first love into sharp focus: "If anyone comes to Me, and does not hate his own father and mother and wife and children and brothers and sisters, yes, and even his own life, he cannot be My disciple" (Luke 14:26).

That is an extremely harsh statement if you take it at face value. But Jesus is not saying you should hate everyone including yourself; He is saying believers must love God and Christ so much that, by comparison, they will seem to hate themselves and their families. If Christians are not willing to put even their closest self-interests far below Christ's interests, that reveals their lack of supreme love to God and that they are not worthy to be called Christ's disciples.

Therefore, if you want to be completely obedient to Christ, there will be times when you need to push aside any and all appeals from family members that would keep you from giving first priority to Him. God might call upon you to make that most difficult of choices to test your loyalty. He wants you to pass the test, even as Abraham did, and thereby prove that He is your first love.

### The Lesson of God's Blessings

There is another purpose in trials and suffering that is very helpful: *they teach us to value the blessing of God.* Trials teach Christians that obedience at all costs, even in the middle of a difficult trial, leads to the blessings of God. Reason says grab what you can grab in the world and go. Sensation and feeling say find pleasure at any price. But faith says obey the Word of God and be blessed.

Jesus illustrates this purpose perfectly in Hebrews 5:7-9:

In the days of His flesh, when He offered up both prayers and supplications with loud crying and tears to Him who was able to save Him from death, and who was heard because of His piety, although He was a Son, He learned obedience from the things which He suffered; and having been made perfect, He became to all those who obey Him the source of eternal salvation.

Philippians 2:8-9 affirms this truth about Jesus in another way: "And being found in the appearance as a man, He humbled Himself by becoming obedient to the point of death, even death on a cross. Therefore also God highly exalted Him, and bestowed on Him the name which is above every name."

Because Jesus was fully man as well as fully God, He was not exempt from pain and hardship while on earth. He was called to be the Suffering Servant (Isa. 53). Jesus learned the full meaning of obedience by that which He suffered, including death on the cross (see again Heb. 5:8), and because of that obedience was exalted by God. The path to blessing is often through suffering, but always through obedience.

### The Lesson of Empathy with Others

One thing all people can appreciate is the ability of others to identify with and understand their particular life situation, problem, unusual experience, or suffering. Whether it's spending time in the hospital and having the doctors and nurses understand the pain you're having, or dealing with a death or disaster and having a sensitive friend know just what you're feeling as you battle through the pressure, it is reassuring when others can empathize with you. And that is another valuable purpose for suffering: *to enable us to help others in their suffering.*

In the opening verses of his second letter to the Corinthians, Paul says that God "comforts us in all our affliction so that we may be able to comfort those who are in any affliction with the comfort with which we ourselves are comforted by God" (1:4). Sometimes God's reason for allowing trials and sufferings to come our way is so we may be able to minister better later on to others who are suffering.

Again the writer of Hebrews tells us how Jesus exemplifies one of the purposes for suffering. Through His own testings and sufferings as the perfect man, Jesus as our High Priest is able to sympathize with our weaknesses and sufferings (2:18; 4:15). He revealed His empathy to Peter during the Last Supper: "Simon, Simon, behold, Satan has demanded permission to sift you like wheat; but I have prayed for you, that your faith may not fail; and you, when once you have turned again, strengthen your brothers" (Luke 22:31-32).

### The Lesson of Enduring Strength

Finally, I believe God allows trials and sufferings *to develop in us enduring strength for greater usefulness.* The Puritan Thomas Manton once said, "While all things are quiet and comfortable, we live by sense rather than faith. But the worth of a soldier is never known in times of peace." The truth of that statement has been borne out many times throughout the history of military conflict, including America's experience with high-tech equipment during the Persian Gulf War.

As the United States built up its forces in the Gulf region in late 1990 to meet the challenge of the Iraqi invasion of Kuwait, questions arose as to how various sophisticated missiles would perform in actual combat situations. These weapons had been experimentally tested only during the previous decade, but the United States had not been involved in a major war (Vietnam) in nearly twenty years. However, much to the relief and satisfaction of military and civilian leaders, the Patriot and cruise missiles performed brilliantly during the two-month Gulf conflict. Those weapons could not be tested to their full worth under training conditions. The pressure of real battlefield conditions and genuine enemy opposition is what proved the missiles' reliability and effectiveness.

Conversely, intense warfare situations also reveal defects in equipment or shortcomings in how troops perform. Based on these observations, improvements can be made. Likewise, the Christian life is a constant warfare (John 17:9-19; Eph. 6:10-18). God places us in difficult life situations to refine us and help us grow (see John 15:1-2). As we move from one trial to another, our spiritual muscles are exercised, strengthened, and become more useful. This whole process builds our spiritual endurance, which makes us all the more effective in future ministry. Remember what the Apostle James teaches us:

> Consider it all joy, my brethren, when you encounter various trials, knowing that the testing of your faith produces endurance. And let endurance have its perfect result, that you may be perfect and complete, lacking in nothing (1:2-4).

The Lord sends trials and sufferings into the Christian's life for various reasons and purposes. Everything from strengthening our faith to reminding us of our heavenly hope to developing enduring strength for greater usefulness may be involved—and God sometimes uses more than one of these purposes at the same time. As we noted at the beginning of the chapter, God is sovereign, and He uses all these worthwhile purposes within the scope of His larger plan for us.

Knowing the wonderful truths in this chapter regarding God's use of trials, sufferings, and persecutions is a comfort, but it is only one aspect of our study. There is still another side to the coin: the difficult and troublesome aspect of application. The practical question that remains is: I know I should triumph through the recognition of God's sovereign purposes in this trial, but what is the path to that triumph? I am willing, but how? And we could ask further, What qualities of mind and emotion are helpful and necessary as we face the situation? The remainder of this book will seek to provide scriptural answers to those questions. We'll begin by looking at some great role models and how they endured suffering in a godly manner.

# TWO

# Examples of Faith in the Fire

We live in an age in which it is common, especially for children and young people, to look for heroes or role models. The audiovisual, mass media culture, which seems to thrive on news and entertainment, constantly rotates people in and out of the celebrity limelight. Some remain there for long periods, others come and go along with particular fads and trends. Many of the personalities in the fields of sports and entertainment are looked up to as role models or worshiped as heroes based on that kind of media recognition. Both Christians and non-Christians admire them because of their success, wealth, intelligence, power, influence, charisma, or some combination of these characteristics. That kind of admiration ignores Paul's questions in 1 Corinthians 1:20, "Where is the wise man? Where is the scribe? Where is the debater of this age? Has not God made foolish the wisdom of the world?" Qualities that are impressive to most of us are rarely the things God sees

as important. Believers today easily forget about looking to Scripture for role models and overlook or avoid
seeking examples of how people from the Bible dealt,
positively and negatively, with sufferings, trials, and
persecutions.

## THE ADVANTAGE OF BIBLICAL ROLE MODELS

As we struggle to live godly lives in the midst of a
hostile world, and in spite of the variety of setbacks
that might discourage us, we need to remember that
believers through the centuries looked to the lives of
great figures in Scripture as their supreme role models.
Historian John Woodbridge writes,

> To whom may we turn for better modeling
> if we are disappointed with the values often
> propagated in the culture at large? Obviously,
> the Christian's foremost model is Jesus Christ
> Himself. The author of the Epistle to the He-
> brews gives us the good counsel to keep our
> eyes fixed upon Him: ". . . let us throw off ev-
> erything that hinders and the sin that so easily
> entangles, and let us run with perseverance
> the race marked out for us." (Hebrews 12:1b-2).
> The same author also provides us with a set
> of role models to reflect upon in his list of men
> and women of faith: Abel, Noah, Abraham, Mo-
> ses, Rahab, David, and others. These biblical
> characters, despite their many weaknesses, tri-
> umphed over enormous adversities through
> their faith (Hebrews 11) (*More Than Conquerors*
> [Chicago: Moody, 1992], 9–10; Scripture quota-
> tion from NIV).

It is easy and natural for us to want to learn from the good characteristics and the successful achievements of the heroes of faith. The "success only" mentality so prevalent in our culture has indeed affected the evangelical church. That is just one among several factors causing believers to miss the whole counsel of God on several key issues.

If we merely study the positive aspects of the lives of biblical role models, we won't see how the power of suffering shaped their characters. I pray that you will gain a balance and grasp some rich insights as we look at some great biblical examples of dealing with sufferings, trials, and persecutions in the next few chapters.

## STEPHEN, THE FIRST CHRISTIAN MARTYR

From the standpoint of seeing his strategic place within God's plan, Stephen's significance was on the same level as Moses'. He played a crucial role during an important transitional time for the early church. It was Stephen's death that resulted in Jerusalem believers being scattered to other parts of the world as witnesses (Acts 8:1). But Stephen's ministry in Acts 6–7, prior to his death, was also crucial. Because he preached to other Greek-speaking Jews in Jerusalem, Stephen became the early church's bridge from Peter, the apostle to the Jews, to Paul, the apostle to the Gentiles. Stephen in effect was the transition between the evangelization of Jerusalem and the evangelization of the world.

Stephen was not only a powerful evangelist, but he was also one of the most articulate defenders of the Christian faith who ever served the church. This is how Luke describes Stephen's ministry:

> And Stephen, full of grace and power, was per-
> forming great wonders and signs among the
> people. But some men from what was called the
> Synagogue of the Freedmen, including both Cy-
> renians and Alexandrians, and some from Cili-
> cia and Asia, rose up and argued with Stephen.
> And yet they were unable to cope with the wis-
> dom and the Spirit with which he was speaking
> (Acts 6:8-10).

Those Greek-speaking Jews were upset with Stephen
because he so convincingly and uncompromisingly set
forth Jesus and the New Covenant as the replacement
for the Jews' Old Covenant religious system. (For a
more complete analysis of Stephen's teaching activity
in Acts 6–7, see my comments in *Acts 1–12*, MacArthur
New Testament Commentary [Chicago: Moody, 1994],
chaps. 15–16.) The Jews' opposition quickly built up to
a level of blind fury that could only be satisfied with
blood—the blood of Stephen as the first Christian martyr (Acts 7:57-60).

Stephen's relatively brief ministry is by itself an inspiration for modern believers. Yet his excellence as a
role model was demonstrated mostly through his
death. We can learn a great deal from his character by
seeing how he responded when confronted by persecution and violent death. Stephen selflessly and courageously did the right thing and proclaimed the truth, in
spite of the consequences.

### Grace in Suffering

In describing the selection of the first deacons, Acts 6:5
calls Stephen "a man full of faith and of the Holy
Spirit." Implicit in the term "faith" is the idea of God's

grace or favor. In fact, Acts 6:8 builds on this phrase from verse 5 and says Stephen was "full of grace and power." Those who have faith and the Spirit—which is all believers—also have a full measure of grace and power. Stephen certainly was filled with all the grace he needed for any situation (see 2 Cor. 12:9; James 4:6; 1 Peter 2:20; 3:14; 4:14).

The kind of grace we're talking about is the grace of loving-kindness toward others, and by faith Stephen definitely had it. That may be part of the reason the Jerusalem church chose him as one of the first deacons, with an initial responsibility to help serve the neglected widows.

Stephen displayed such grace toward others in a far more powerful way just before he died. In Acts 7:60 while the Jews were stoning him, smashing rocks against his head and body, Stephen knelt, looked up to heaven, and exclaimed, "Lord, do not hold this sin against them!" Such graciousness can come only from the Lord. How else could a human being bestow such favorable words upon those who were killing him? This kind of faith-filled, grace-filled response by Stephen was the result of his belief that God was sovereignly in control of his life and death. That's why Stephen didn't worry about protecting himself; he died happily and peacefully in God's will. He simply trusted in God's overall plan for him and didn't fight back to save himself (compare Gen. 50:20; Jer. 29:11).

### Serenity in Suffering

Near the beginning of his fatal persecution at the hands of the unbelieving Jews, Stephen displayed another clear and remarkable signal that the episode was not an ordinary one. Acts 6:15 says, "And fixing their gaze on him, all who were sitting in the Council saw his face like the face of an angel." His facial expression must have been one of the most incomprehensible yet wonderful rebukes ever set forth against such vicious, lying, ungodly intimidation and persecution. Surely Stephen's opponents were astounded and confounded by such an untypical reaction. The normal human response, which many believers might exhibit in a similar situation, would have included anxiety, stress, and perhaps anger.

Stephen's extraordinary godly response to his unjust treatment ("they came upon him and dragged him away," v. 12) and the distorted, false charges (v. 11) hurled at him, gives us further example of how to behave in the middle of the most difficult of circumstances. The serene and composed expression on Stephen's face provides more proof that he was Spirit-filled and had an intimate relationship with God.

We can't know exactly how Stephen's angelic face would have looked, but I believe he essentially manifested a supernatural tranquility and joy as a result of being engulfed by the glory of God's presence. The Apostle Peter says, "If you are reviled for the name of Christ, you are blessed, because the Spirit of glory and of God rests upon you" (1 Peter 4:14). Stephen had radiating from his face the glory of God, which is why his expression was such an incredible rebuke to those unbelieving Jews, who claimed to know God.

The other man who reflected the glory of God on his face was Moses (Ex. 33:7-11, 17-23; 34:29-35). The irony of this for Stephen's foes was that even as they falsely charged him with blasphemy against Moses, God was immediately reflecting His glory from Stephen's face (Acts 6:11-15). That effectively placed Stephen on a par with Moses (we alluded to this earlier in the chapter) and revealed that God approved of Stephen as a messenger of the New Covenant. At the appropriate time God had approved of Moses as the representative of the Old Covenant, but now it was Stephen's turn as a representative of Christ (see 2 Cor. 3:7-11).

### Godliness in Suffering

One thread of truth that has run explicitly and implicitly through our short study of Stephen is his high level of godliness. We have already seen in Acts 6:5 that he was filled with the Holy Spirit. He is also described that way in Acts 7:55, after his sermon and just as the Jews, in their extreme rage of unbelief, are about to seize him for the last time. The reality of being filled with the Spirit has great application for us as we consider coping with suffering and persecution in our lives.

Acts 7:55 says, "But being full of the Holy Spirit, he gazed intently into heaven and saw the glory of God, and Jesus standing at the right hand of God." The *New American Standard* translation, rendered here "being full," from a verb form of the Greek *pleroō*, provides a good clue to the meaning of being filled with the Spirit. Literally, Stephen was being continuously filled with (or full of) the Holy Spirit. He was full of the Holy Spirit in Acts 6, that's why the church chose him as a deacon. He was constantly being filled with the Spirit as he ministered. And he was still full of the Spirit at the end of Acts 7. This understanding of filling as a continuous action agrees with Paul's command in the second part of Ephesians 5:18, "but be filled with the Spirit." Here the Greek *pleroō* should be translated literally "being kept filled." All Christians are to be con-

tinually filled with and thus controlled by the Holy
Spirit.

Because there is so much confusion, misunderstanding, and false teaching today regarding the full-
ness of the Spirit in the believer's life, we need to elaborate just a bit more on the Holy Spirit's role. A
computer-related adage says, "Garbage in, garbage
out." In a similar way, we are controlled by what fills
our minds. If we let the Holy Spirit control our minds,
we'll be controlled and renewed by Him and we'll exhibit godly behavior. The command in Ephesians 5:18
does not mean to have some kind of mystical experience. It simply means believers should let their lives be
controlled by the Spirit of God. *Pleroō* is often used in
the Gospels to mean be filled with a certain attitude,
like anger or bitterness. Generally we are able to keep a
balance between anger and happiness. But if we become filled with anger we lose that balance and become
dominated by anger. Likewise, if we are Christians we
are to be controlled by the Spirit.

Stephen, in keeping with his status as an excellent
role model, fit the ideal of one totally and continuously
filled and controlled by the Spirit. He didn't have to
make any adjustments or take a final few moments to
take a spiritual inventory when he saw he was going to
die. He had apparently lived a consistent, Spirit-filled
life ever since he became a believer. Therefore, it was
natural for Stephen to react in a godly, trusting fashion
in the face of persecution and death. And we should be
able to handle suffering today—which is usually much
less intense—in the same manner because the same
Holy Spirit is in us as was in Stephen.

The problem for us may be that we don't believe
we can handle a crisis situation like Stephen's. But such

doubting is unjustified. Look again at 1 Peter 4:14 where Peter says in response to persecution that "you are blessed, because the Spirit of glory and of God rests upon you." We can infer from this that God provides for us in a special way when we are severely tested or persecuted. It's as if His Spirit were poured out in a double portion at the time of crisis. Certainly that's what happened to Stephen in Acts 7, to countless thousands of other martyrs throughout church history, and to you and me when we face difficulties. God is more than adequate to meet all our needs at such times (Phil. 4:13). That's why we have no logical reason to fear or shrink back at the prospect of suffering for Christ's sake.

One further piece of evidence demonstrating Stephen's godliness in persecution was his twofold response in Acts 7:55-56. He looked to Jesus and confidently testified that he saw Him standing at the right hand of God. He looked away from his tough circumstances and fixed his eyes on Jesus. That previews Paul's exhortation: "If then you have been raised up with Christ, keep seeking the things above, where Christ is, seated at the right hand of God. Set your mind on the things above, not on the things that are on earth" (Col. 3:1-2).

Stephen's spiritual sight was incredible, no doubt as a result of his being "full of faith and of the Holy Spirit." That sight enabled him to have a revelation of the risen Savior and to know for sure that he would be received into heaven the moment he died. We won't experience such a revelation or vision of Jesus in this life, but by the eyes of faith we can always see Him and know He is with us in the most trying of times (John 14:26-27; Acts 2:24-25; Heb. 13:5-6).

Stephen, despite his very short ministry career, ranks with the giants of the faith. Perhaps only the Lord Jesus, the perfect role model, and Paul (2 Cor. 11:23-31) could surpass Stephen as a model for how to deal with suffering. Stephen definitely adhered to the following words of David from centuries earlier:

> I have set the Lord continually before me; because He is at my right hand, I will not be shaken. Therefore my heart is glad, and my glory rejoices; my flesh also will dwell securely. For Thou wilt not abandon my soul to Sheol; neither wilt Thou allow Thy Holy One to see the pit. Thou wilt make known to me the path of life; in Thy presence is fulness of joy; in Thy right hand there are pleasures forever (Ps. 16:8-11).

## DANIEL AND HIS THREE FRIENDS

The Book of Daniel is one of the most critical in the Old Testament, since it deals with many visions and prophecies of the end times. But it also contains much valuable historical material that has direct application to our lives. The historical narrative focuses on four Jewish young men who were among the exiles in Babylon: Daniel (the author and main character of the book) and his three friends Hananiah, Mishael, and Azariah (better known by their Chaldean names Shadrach, Meshach, and Abed-nego). These men were leading players in some of the most familiar Bible stories that provide important insight to our study of role models and suffering.

In one of his textbooks an eminent naturalist describes a marine plant that grows from a depth of 150 to 200 feet and floats on the ocean breakers. The stem of this plant is less than an inch thick, yet it grows and holds its own against the fierce poundings of the breakers that crash against the shore. What is the key to this seemingly frail plant's marvelous endurance and its resistance to the pressure of the waves? According to the naturalist the slender plant survives so well against the elements because it is anchored solidly to the rocks that lie at the bottom of the water.

It's amazing how believers can endure the crushing blows of life's breakers if they also have a proper anchor. No matter how weak our faith may seem, when it is anchored to the unfailing promises of God's Word, we can withstand the strongest buffeting and the most difficult suffering. In the case of Daniel and his friends, we can see that though their feet were planted in Babylon, their heads were in heaven. Their hearts and minds were firmly committed to God's absolutes and thus they were willing and able to stand up to and resist the pressures of a pagan society.

### The Furnace and Daniel's Friends

In the struggle that is the Christian life we need to decide, based on God's Word, what is essential and what is nonessential. We need to come to the place where we can draw the line of conviction and determine not to fall below it. In this way we can operate from the strength of internal principle rather than the intimidation of external pressure in times of crisis and trouble.

Daniel and his friends had drawn such a line of conviction early in their time in Babylon (Dan. 1:8). They determined not to vacillate when it came to the absolutes of the law and the Word of God, and that decision anchored them to God, their rock of confidence, and allowed them to endure all the storms of the Chaldean-Babylonian Captivity.

The Babylonian exile of the Jews began around 606 B.C. Daniel and his friends were among the first group of Jews deported to Babylon after Nebuchadnezzar's initial invasion of Judah. They were taken, along with many other of the finest young men of Judah, as hostages to be trained in Chaldean culture to act as leaders of the Jewish captives. This leadership would prevent the Jews from revolting against the Babylonian takeover. The men were selected on the basis of physical and intellectual prowess and social graces. The Babylonians wanted to groom the men for service in their courts. Actually, it was more a matter of reeducation, redefinition of identity, and reorientation of lifestyle— in essence, brainwashing.

The men did not resist the educational process or the changing of their names, but they did resist the attempt to reorient them to a pagan lifestyle. The reason for this was very clear. There was no biblical mandate against receiving a new education or changing their names, but there was a clear scriptural mandate that prevented them from adopting the lifestyle of Babylon. For example, they could not eat some of the Chaldean foods because that would violate certain absolute statements in the law of God about diet and food offered to idols. So Daniel and his three friends drew the line where God had drawn it. They knew precisely the boundary beyond which they could not and would not go.

Daniel and his friends, because they behaved consistently yet graciously according to their convictions,

earned a large measure of favor and respect from Nebuchadnezzar. They had heeded well the words of Proverbs 22:11, "He who loves purity of heart and whose
speech is gracious, the king is his friend." However,
such friendship proved to be short-lived.

Certain events described in Daniel 3 confront Daniel's three friends with a very agonizing dilemma—a
much more trying crisis of character than dietary restrictions (Dan. 1:8-16). Here the issue involves idolatry
and giving God first place in worship. The three young
men knew that God's law was clear-cut: considering
any object of worship as greater than God was heinous
in His sight (Ex. 20:2-6; Deut. 4:15-19).

In Daniel 2:31-35, Nebuchadnezzar dreamed of an
impressive, large statue with a head of solid gold and a
body of silver, bronze, iron, and clay. He was so captivated by that gold head, which represented himself (v.
38), that he commissioned his own massive, solid gold
statue to be built (3:1). The entire project was completely self-serving for Nebuchadnezzar: the giant image
represented himself and his monarchy. He was simply
doing what all men tend to do who don't know God,
namely, worshiping himself as a god. And in this case
Nebuchadnezzar demanded that all his subjects bow
down to him—and they did, except for the three men.
They stood resolutely on internal principle, based on
God's Word, at the risk of death: "Whoever does not
fall down and worship shall immediately be cast into
the midst of a furnace of blazing fire" (v. 6).

This act of conviction, which is at first merely inferred from the text of Daniel 3, exposed the three
young men to fierce opposition and persecution from
the Chaldeans. The Chaldeans were already resentful
toward Daniel and his three friends for having been

given government positions ahead of them (2:48-49). Daniel 3:12 summarizes their accusations against Daniel's colleagues: "There are certain Jews whom you have appointed over the administration of the province of Babylon, namely Shadrach, Meshach, and Abednego. These men, O king, have disregarded you; they do not serve your gods or worship the golden image which you have set up."

Upon hearing this charge, King Nebuchadnezzar went into a rage and ordered the three brought to him. As if the men did not face enough pressure, they were subjected to a last-ditch, prideful attempt to force them to conform to the king's order.

The men did not really need to answer Nebuchadnezzar's threats and intimidations, and for the most part they didn't. Their composure and quiet strength of character would have been sufficient as their only response. Their silence was not arrogance, but a tacit admission that the charge of not worshiping the golden image was true. They realized there was no need to waste time rationalizing their behavior or conducting an elaborate self-defense. Instead, they uttered one of the most concise yet sublime statements of faith in all of Scripture:

> If it be so, our God whom we serve is able to deliver us from the furnace of blazing fire; and He will deliver us out of your hand, O king. But even if He does not, let it be known to you, O king, that we are not going to serve your gods or worship the golden image that you have set up (Dan. 3:17-18).

Once again we see the concept of internal principle at work with the three young men. First they placed principle so high that they were able to stand up while everyone else in the massive crowd bowed to the golden image. That enabled them to resist the external peer pressure that says, "Go ahead. What does it matter in the long run? Everyone else is doing it." Second, they anchored their internal principle upon God and His Word (Ps. 119:11). They knew that what happened to their bodies was not the issue but that their souls had to be riveted on the truth of God. Like Job they said, "Though He slay me, I will hope in Him" (Job 13:15).

The courageous stand of Shadrach, Meshach, and Abed-nego was soon put to the extreme test in the fiery furnace. From Nebuchadnezzar's stubborn resistance to their statement, it quickly became evident that God was not going to keep them out of the fire. They now had to hope that their deliverance, if that was God's will, would come from within the furnace. Perhaps they were remembering the words of the Lord from Isaiah 43:2, "When you walk through the fire, you will not be scorched, nor will the flame burn you."

The brave, high-principled stand taken by the three men led to the Lord's miraculous intervention. Daniel 3:24-25 tells us that Nebuchadnezzar sees a fourth man in the flames. He may have been a preincarnate appearance of Christ (cf. Gen. 18:1-3) or he may have been an angel. We can infer from the passage that he was a messenger from God sent to preserve the men in the midst of the fire.

Daniel's three cohorts are an extraordinary testimony of how inner principle and conviction, grounded in the truth of God, can prepare believers for and sustain them through the greatest of persecutions and testings. These three men received the added blessing of avoiding physical harm, even though they were in the middle of conditions that normally result in instantaneous death.

Their testimony was so unusual and so powerful that pagan King Nebuchadnezzar gave glory to God: "Blessed be the God of Shadrach, Meshach, and Abed-nego, who has sent His angel and delivered His servants who put their trust in Him, violating the king's command, and yielded up their bodies so as not to serve or worship any god except their own God" (Dan. 3:28). Notice the phrase "yielded up their bodies." That is an amazing foreshadowing, out of the mouth of an unbelieving king, of the Apostle Paul's words in Romans 12:1-2,

> I urge you therefore, brethren, by the mercies of God, to present your bodies a living and holy sacrifice, acceptable to God, which is your spiritual service of worship. And do not be conformed to this world, but be transformed by the renewing of your mind, that you may prove what the will of God is, that which is good and acceptable and perfect.

Shadrach, Meshach, and Abed-nego were themselves forerunners of all believers from the New Testament until now who have sought to be men and women of inner conviction and consistent disciples in the Romans 12 pattern. They are also excellent role models for us as we anticipate adversity in this world.

### Daniel in the Lions' Den
Daniel had served as somewhat of a mentor for his three friends. That role could imply superiority of rank and exemption from the kinds of hardships and pres-

sures his friends endured. In fact, Daniel is not mentioned in the narrative about the fiery furnace and the golden image. But years later in God's sovereign plan, Daniel himself would find his life in jeopardy because of his convictions. He also became the target of jealous schemers who hated righteousness.

Daniel 6 indicates that he had continued on the road of excellence in his character and government service: "Daniel began distinguishing himself among the commissioners and satraps because he possessed an extraordinary spirit, and the king planned to appoint him over the entire kingdom" (6:3). The "extraordinary spirit" refers to Daniel's ability to interpret dreams and visions, but it can also remind us of his consistently high standards of spiritual conduct and attitude.

There is usually a price to pay for being in a position of blessing and prominence in ministry. The Apostle Paul was continually dogged by false teachers who wanted to undo his work in the churches (cf. Acts 20:29-32) and by those who were envious (Phil. 1:12-20). While Paul was in prison some of his enemies wanted to make his situation worse by claiming evil things about his ministry. Certain people even went so far as to preach Christ contentiously in an effort to undermine Paul. It is amazing and troubling how others can have so much rage, jealousy, and bitterness against leaders who have done nothing to offend or harm them. How could his contemporaries possibly hate Daniel? They certainly could not find any basis in his character.

When Daniel's opponents began plotting against him they had to look beyond the areas of earthly concern and government service: "We shall not find any ground of accusation against this Daniel unless we find it against him with regard to the law of his God" (Dan. 6:5). To accuse him, Daniel's foes had to persecute him for righteousness' sake. What a commendation it was for Daniel that his enemies could not find fault with him for anything except his total commitment to his God.

The conspiracy against Daniel culminated when his adversaries contrived to pass a new law dealing with one's loyalty to the king and deities. They even persuaded King Darius, who had by then taken Nebuchadnezzar's throne, to make it an irrevocable injunction, according to the famous law of the Medes and Persians. This new law made the king supreme, almost as a deity, and everyone was forbidden to petition any god or man but him, at the penalty of death. Of course this concept was targeted especially at Daniel, but it would leave him undaunted in his obedience to God.

The text tells us Daniel persevered in doing the right thing: "Now when Daniel knew that the document was signed, he entered his house (now in his roof chamber he had windows open toward Jerusalem); and he continued kneeling on his knees three times a day, praying and giving thanks before his God, as he had been doing previously" (v. 10). Daniel persevered without regard to the consequences of the new law. That attitude parallels that of Peter and John when they refused to stop proclaiming the good news of Christ (Acts 4:17-21).

Daniel could have cut corners and been more discreet in his daily spiritual disciplines, but he didn't. He could have compromised, omitting his daily prayer to God for the next thirty days, but he didn't. Any compromise at all would have been seen as self-serving, and that simply was not part of Daniel's character. His faithful resolve reminds me of the story of Polycarp, one of the great early church fathers, who was martyred in A.D. 155, having been a Christian for eighty-six years. As his enemies prepared to burn him at the stake in Smyrna, they gave him one last chance to deny the Lord and save his life. Polycarp responded with quiet assurance and a steady voice, "Eighty-six years have I served Him, He's never done me any harm; why should I forsake Him now?" With that expression of commitment to Christ he accepted the flames as God's will and died with praises on his lips.

Daniel did not deviate from his former pattern of personal prayer and devotion. Ultimately his enemies caught him, and they reported him to the king. Following the exposure of Daniel's disobedience to the new decree, it is interesting to note that Scripture records nothing of what he may have said or done in his defense. Presumably there was nothing for him to say— he had such confidence in God through all the years that he simply committed himself to Him.

Surprisingly this passage portrays King Darius as having the most active and vocal concern about Daniel's fate. In spite of his reluctance, and only after a futile attempt to find some loophole in the new law, Darius had to bow to the pressure of Daniel's enemies and throw him into the lions' den, which was the means of implementing the death penalty. However, as the king carried out his grim obligation, he said to Daniel: "Your God whom you constantly serve will Himself deliver you" (v. 16). That suggests Darius had been significantly influenced by Daniel's life and ministry and was willing to give credit to the true God, which is all that Daniel would have desired. Daniel's previous testimony in various situations—regarding dietary requirements, interpreting several visions—was paying rich dividends now and allowing him to remain silent in front of the king.

Daniel did not speak again until after God had the opportunity to show His might once again and deliver Daniel from the lions. In a sense Daniel allowed the sovereign course of events to vindicate first God and then himself (vv. 17-22). The words of verse 23 summarize the outcome of this familiar account: "Then the king was very pleased and gave orders for Daniel to be taken up out of the den. So Daniel was taken up out of the den, and no injury whatever was found on him, because he had trusted in his God."

We began this chapter by affirming the importance of biblical role models as godly patterns for how to behave in both good times and bad times. In this era of church history, with its emphasis on positive self-image, successful Christian living, and feeling good about whatever works to build the church, believers tend to look to themselves or contemporary role models for strength and inspiration. While there are contemporary Christian role models, none can substitute for biblical personalities who dealt so nobly and courageously with adversity.

There are similarities and differences among the three case studies in this chapter: These men faced varying amounts of opposition from their unbelieving foes, but only Stephen was asked to suffer physical pain and death as a result of his ordeal. Yet one theme stands out in all three studies: Each individual exhibited strong faith and resolution of purpose. Of course, the object of their faith was God. Their strong faith, which was not developed in a vacuum, produced another common characteristic: a calmness and patient reliance upon a sovereign God to sustain them through the time of crisis. Those traits were repeated in the testimonies of Daniel and his friends as they leaned upon internal principles. Stephen and the men in Daniel were prepared for the trials and sufferings that eventually confronted them.

Once we have overcome our tendency to avoid or deny the existence of sufferings or trials, we can begin to see that it is possible for us also to deal with any kind of suffering. We serve the same God as Stephen, Daniel, Shadrach, Meshach, and Abed-nego. They are superior examples of believers who cultivated a godly life style and resolutely put God first, not looking to the right or to the left. Those traits prepared them well for the tests and sufferings they endured. They genuinely fit the pattern of Hebrews 12:1-2,

> Therefore, since we have so great a cloud of witnesses surrounding us, let us also lay aside every encumbrance, and the sin which so easily entangles us, and let us run with endurance the race that is set before us, fixing our eyes on Jesus, the author and perfecter of faith, who for the joy set before Him endured the cross, despising the shame, and has sat down at the right hand of the throne of God.

Examples from Scripture history ought to motivate and encourage us. And that motivation is ours by faith in Christ, not by some complicated, mysterious methodology that was available only to believers such as Stephen or Daniel. We too can experience the benefits of the power of suffering in our lives without anxiety and dread. This confidence grows as we simply, on a daily basis, realize that we as Christians are "full of faith and of the Holy Spirit."

# THREE

# *Paul:*
# *A Profile in Suffering*

Many scholars believe the Apostle Paul was the kind of person who would have gained some significant niche in secular history even if he had not been converted to Christ. As Saul of Tarsus, a prominent Pharisee with a brilliant intellect and strong leadership traits, he already had the potential for leaving a lasting mark on the first-century Mediterranean world. Paul was by any measure the most spiritually influential person who ever lived. Certainly believers who love God's Word know that Paul is second only to the Lord Jesus as the dominant figure in the New Testament. Twenty of the twenty-eight chapters in the Book of Acts chronicle Paul's life, including his conversion, early ministry, and missionary journeys. The Holy Spirit used him more than any of the other apostles as an author of thirteen New Testament books. Christ's life and work are thoroughly interpreted in his letters, and all believers throughout the centuries have found in his epistles the truth that transforms lives.

It is for those very reasons that we look now to Paul as another role model of coping with suffering. Paul even held himself up as an example to the churches—he had the Spirit-inspired confidence to urge the Corinthians, "Be imitators of me, just as I also am of Christ" (1 Cor. 11:1; see also 4:16; Phil. 3:17).

Paul certainly was a worthy example of Christian discipleship in all its various facets (Acts 20:18-35; Phil. 3:1-16; 1 Thes. 2:1-12). However, Paul's career as an apostle and pioneering church planter was not one always marked by easy progress. More than any of the other apostles, he knew the meaning of suffering and adversity. Herbert Lockyer says this:

> As you follow Paul from country to country (Rom. 15:19), mark how he suffered for Christ's sake in his missionary labors. Here is a list for you to ponder over with your open Bible—
>
> Enduring every species of hardship, encountering every extreme danger (II Cor. 11:23-27). Assaulted by the populace, punished by magistrates (Acts 16:19-24; 21:27). Scourged, beaten, stoned, left for dead (Acts 14:19-20). Expecting wherever he went a renewal of the same treatment and the same dangers (Acts 20:23). Driven from one city, he preached in the next (Acts 13:50-51; 14:5-7, 19-21). Spent his whole time in missionary work, sacrificing to it his pleasures, his ease, his safety (Acts 20:24; Rom. 1:14-15; Phil. 1:20; 3:8). Persisted in this course to old age, unaltered by the experience of perverseness (Acts 28:17); ingratitude (Gal. 1:6; 4:14-20); prejudice (II Cor. 12:15); and desertion (II Tim. 4:10, 16). Unsubdued by anxiety, want, labor, or

persecution, unwearied by long confinement, undismayed by the prospect of death (Acts 21:13; II Cor. 12:10; Phil. 2:17; 4:18; II Tim. 4:17).

At his conversion, Paul was warned of the many things he would have to suffer for Christ's sake (Acts 9:16), and as he came to suffer he never sighed or moaned but gloried in his tribulations and was prouder of his scars in battle than a soldier of his medals and decorations (Gal. 6:17). What a warrior-missionary he was! The world has never seen his like (*All the Apostles of the Bible* [Grand Rapids: Zondervan, 1972], 219–20).

## KNOWING JOY AMID SUFFERING

Joy is one of the fruits of the Spirit-controlled life, according to Galatians 5:22, "But the fruit of the Spirit is love, joy, peace, patience, kindness, goodness, faithfulness." We are commanded to rejoice at all times and in all things: "Rejoice in the Lord always; again I will say, rejoice!" (Phil. 4:4); "Rejoice always" (1 Thes. 5:16). There is really only one justification for believers to lose their joy, and that is when they sin. Consider what David said in the aftermath of his sin: "Restore to me the joy of Thy salvation" (Ps. 51:12).

We should never forfeit our joy to sullenness, bitterness, or negativism simply because things aren't the way we would like them to be. Nevertheless, it is typical for believers to let the changing circumstances of difficulties, confusions, trials, economic troubles, attacks, disagreements, unfulfilled expectations or ambitions, strained relationships, and so forth throw them off balance and steal their joy.

In chapter 1 we examined the rationale for believers experiencing trials and sufferings, concluding that they should expect them and believe that the Lord has a good and glorious purpose for them. In the midst of any difficult circumstance is the struggle of maintaining our joy. The Apostle Paul is a larger-than-life model of success in that struggle. The New Testament does not record Paul allowing any circumstance to take away his joy in the Lord. On the contrary, the greater the adversity the more insistent he was to articulate his joy.

Paul had joy in spite of difficult opposition because his overriding purpose and focus was to see the cause of Christ furthered. Three aspects, derived from his letter to the Philippians, show how Paul was an example of maintaining his joy in the middle of trials and suffering.

### Joy in Spite of Trouble

Paul wrote to the Philippians as a prisoner in Rome during his second two-year imprisonment (he had already languished for two years in Caesarea before being shipped to Rome). Romans 1:10 indicates Paul's original feeling regarding his earnest desire to come to Rome: "if by any means now at length I might have a prosperous journey by the will of God to come unto you" (KJV). However, he did not have the prosperous journey he might have wished or prayed for. Rather, it was God's will that he arrive in Rome as a prisoner.

Paul had been given a preliminary hearing (alluded to in Phil. 1:7) after arriving in Rome. He was then awaiting a decision from Emperor Nero on whether he would be executed or released. During this waiting period, Paul had some unusual conditions associated with his imprisonment. He was not housed with the rest of the prisoners but was allowed to stay by himself, chained to the soldier who was guarding him. Acts 28:30-31 elaborates: "And he stayed two full years in his own rented quarters, and was welcoming all who came to him, preaching the kingdom of God, and teaching concerning the Lord Jesus Christ with all openness, unhindered." Even though he had some amount of freedom to speak the Gospel and see various people, Paul was still basically a prisoner with all the characteristic restrictions.

After not hearing from Paul for four years, the Philippians discovered that Paul was being held as a prisoner in Rome. Because of their previous close bond with him, they naturally wanted to know what was happening. To accomplish that, they sent Epaphroditus to discover how Paul was doing and how the Gospel was faring. The answer to these questions constitutes the core of the letter to the Philippians.

In the Philippian correspondence Paul essentially lets his readers know that in spite of circumstances he was rejoicing. Although his conditions were hard and threatening, and no doubt disappointing for the Philippian believers to read about, the Gospel was still going forward, even among the guards. The key that allowed Paul to rejoice was his ability to see beyond himself and the pains, restrictions, and inconveniences of his circumstances. His greatest priority was the advancement of Christ's Gospel, not a concern for his own comfort (see Acts 20:24; Rom. 1:15; 1 Cor. 9:16).

Because he saw himself as a prisoner for the sake of Christ, Paul did not wallow in self-pity. Instead he viewed himself as a servant or soldier on duty for the greater cause of spreading the good news of Jesus Christ. Paul mentions his imprisonment often in his

letters (Eph. 3:1; Col. 4:10, 18; Phile. 1, 9), and always in
a positive light because he connected it with the cause
of Christ.

Perhaps the most dramatic illustration of Paul's ability to rejoice in spite of suffering and imprisonment took
place at an earlier time in a prison in Philippi:

> And the crowd rose up together against them,
> and the chief magistrates tore their robes off
> them, and proceeded to order them to be beat-
> en with rods. And when they had inflicted
> many blows upon them, they threw them into
> prison, commanding the jailer to guard them
> securely; and he, having received such a com-
> mand, threw them into the inner prison, and
> fastened their feet in the stocks. But about mid-
> night Paul and Silas were praying and singing
> hymns of praise to God, and the prisoners were
> listening to them; and suddenly there came a
> great earthquake, so that the foundations of the
> prison house were shaken; and immediately all
> the doors were opened, and everyone's chains
> were unfastened. And when the jailer had been
> roused out of sleep and had seen the prison
> doors opened, he drew his sword and was about
> to kill himself, supposing that the prisoners had
> escaped. But Paul cried out with a loud voice,
> saying, "Do yourself no harm, for we are all
> here!" And he called for lights and rushed in
> and, trembling with fear, he fell down before
> Paul and Silas, and after he brought them out,
> he said, "Sirs, what must I do to be saved?"
> And they said, "Believe in the Lord Jesus, and
> you shall be saved, you and your household."

> And they spoke the word of the Lord to him
> together with all who were in his house. And
> he took them that very hour of the night and
> washed their wounds, and immediately he was
> baptized, he and all his household (Acts 16:22-
> 33).

Given the situation, that was an incredible display of
joy in the face of adversity. Ancient prisons like the one
at Philippi were dark and dingy, unclean and unsani-
tary. In addition, Paul and Silas had their arms and legs
stretched out wide and then locked in the stocks while
still suffering the wounds from their beatings. Yet Paul
describes himself as rejoicing in the middle of such
torture.

In this episode with the Philippian jailer Paul illustrates how he so often took advantage of opportunities
within times of adversity to spread the Gospel. This
evangelizing could easily be seen as an overflow of
Paul's joyful attitude. He again seized the opportunity,
this time among the guards, during his Roman imprisonment: "My imprisonment in the cause of Christ has
become well-known throughout the whole praetorian
guard and to everyone else" (Phil. 1:13). Evidently his
efforts were fruitful: "All the saints greet you, especially
those of Caesar's household [the guards]" (4:22).

Based on the context, it wasn't just Paul's ability to
articulate the Gospel that had an impact on the guards,
nor was it his gracious, merciful demeanor. Ultimately
he made an impact because the truth he spoke and the
godly character he exhibited were ingrained in a man
experiencing deep affliction. What a tremendous lesson
that is to us today (see 1 Peter 3:15). If you are currently
facing a difficult witnessing situation either at work or

at home, you can actually turn that into an easier process by demonstrating Christlikeness and godly character traits throughout the adversity. Your attitude will stand in sharp contrast with what others naturally expect from you, and will create opportunities for testifying to God's glory and grace.

### Joy in Spite of Detractors

Throughout church history the most difficult opposition for the church has typically come from within or from those who profess to be religious. The specific opposition or persecution is not as distressing as is the disappointment of receiving unexpected criticism and attack from those you thought were supporters. Paul, however, rises above such disappointment and discouragement while contending with detractors from the ranks of other preachers during his stay in prison. He shows joy in spite of apparent difficulties because he knows the Gospel is advancing.

The dictionary defines detraction as "the uttering of material (as false or slanderous charges) that is likely to damage the reputation of another." A detractor is someone who wants to undercut and tear down the character or reputation of someone else—and there were plenty of such people attacking Paul. From our modern vantage point it is hard to believe that a man like Paul, who was so godly, faithful, and dedicated to the cause of Christ, could have faced such serious detractors from within the church. But that kind of opposition has been characteristic of prominent leaders throughout history. Even Abraham Lincoln, who is universally considered one of the greatest American Presidents ever, was severely criticized and viciously attacked by political opponents and by unsympathetic newspaper editors during the height of the American Civil War.

Philippians 1:15 identifies Paul's chief detractors: "Some, to be sure, are preaching Christ even from envy and strife." These men were Paul's fellow preachers who proclaimed the same Gospel as Paul. Doctrinal differences were not the cause of their opposition to Paul, but personal differences—specifically the sinful motives of envy and strife associated with their preaching. Simply put, they were jealous of Paul's gifts and blessings from God in addition to the large following he had attracted from the many converts God had given him and the churches he had founded and ministered to.

In his letter Paul refers to those detractors not to garner sympathy for himself, but to inform the Philippians about this crucial time in his ministry. He was not retaliating against his critics—that would not be consistent with his standard response to difficulties. One aspect of that response was to accept opposition patiently and turn it from a negative to a positive.

Paul undoubtedly gained patience from his experience in dealing with disappointments and letdowns caused by other would-be supporters (see 2 Tim. 1:15; 4:16). Having to contend with this latest group of detractors was just one more trial in a long list. Paul elaborates some more in Philippians 1:17 about the methods his detractors used: "The former proclaim Christ out of selfish ambition, rather than from pure motives, thinking to cause me distress in my imprisonment." The word "distress" is the translation of the Greek *thlipsis*, which basically means "friction." Paul's foes attempted to inflict extra irritation on him while he was in prison. Their malicious goal was to discredit him in the eyes of his followers so he would lose all credibility.

However much Paul's jealous detractors may have succeeded in shaking the confidence and faith of some in the churches, they were not able to shake Paul. He withstood all the ugliness that was hurled at him and was able to conclude, "What then? Only that in every way, whether in pretense or in truth, Christ is proclaimed; and in this I rejoice, yes, and I will rejoice" (Phil. 1:18). In spite of it all, they could not steal his joy because he knew Christ's cause was being furthered.

The lesson for all of us from Paul's example is very clear: we need not allow any amount of unfair or false treatment to steal our joy in Christ and the Gospel. The key for us to emulate, by God's power, is Paul's intense, overriding devotion to the cause of Jesus Christ (cf. Rom. 8:28-39; Phil. 3:7-14).

## Joy in Spite of Death

One great certainty that everyone faces is death, whether it arrives unexpectedly or approaches slowly, allowing its victim time to prepare for the inevitable. Of course, not all people accept the unexpected prognosis of death with equal calmness, peace of mind, and even joy.

A poignant but heartwarming illustration of how one person was coping scripturally with a terminal illness came to the attention of my radio ministry recently. A high school girl from the Midwest sent a prayer request to us in which she told of being diagnosed with Lou Gehrig's disease just a few weeks earlier. This Christian young woman, who had been given six months to two years to live, accepted the reality of her condition with grace and optimism, as demonstrated by these comments: "I love the Lord very much and feel the Lord is using my condition to work in different peoples' lives. Please pray with me that He would continue to use me no matter what the outcome."

In Philippians 1:19-21 Paul expresses a strong level of confidence and joy regarding his possible death:

> For I know that this shall turn out for my deliverance through your prayers and the provision of the Spirit of Jesus Christ, according to my earnest expectation and hope, that I shall not be put to shame in anything, but that with all boldness, Christ shall even now, as always, be exalted in my body, whether by life or by death. For to me, to live is Christ, and to die is gain.

Paul was a living illustration of a disciple who was willing to take up his cross for the Gospel's sake (Matt. 16:24-25). He exhibited a high level of spiritual commitment—one that is not often seen in the church in our materialistic, self-centered, self-serving age. Paul was confident of four things that helped him face death without fear. A brief examination of each can help us in our own struggles as we seek to be better prepared for sufferings and trials.

*Confidence in God's Word.* Paul's statement "For I know that this shall turn out for my deliverance" is a verbatim quote from Job 13:16 in the Greek Old Testament. The word "know" is from the Greek *oida*, which means "to know for a certainty." Paul is expressing a sure confidence in what is going to happen.

Paul could be certain of his deliverance because he had confidence in God's promises. In Romans 8:28 he writes, "We know that God causes all things to work together for good to those who love God, to those who are called according to His purpose." Paul quoted from the Book of Job to the Philippians because he knew that that statement also was a promise from God. Paul also identified with the struggles and sufferings that Job endured.

Paul believed, as Job did, that his trials and hardships were merely temporary. Whether the suffering would be for a short season or a long one, Paul knew God would deliver him because he was righteous—a principle that God established in the Old Testament (Pss. 34:17, 19; 37:39-40; 91:3; 97:10). Furthermore, he was well-acquainted with how God rescued and restored Job from a difficult time of suffering.

We can have the same confidence in the face of death as Paul or Job had, and more so, because we possess the entire written Scripture. We can "keep on rejoicing" if God calls us to face suffering or death for His sake (1 Peter 4:13).

*Confidence in the Prayers of the Saints.* Paul believed in the eternal purposes of God that He established from before time began, but he also knew that God did His work and accomplished His purposes in association with the prayers of believers.

Paul, however, did not allow his confidence in prayer to become presumptuous. He believed in asking people to pray for him: "Now I urge you, brethren, by our Lord Jesus Christ and by the love of the Spirit, to strive together with me in your prayers to God for me" (Rom. 15:30; see also Eph. 6:19). Once he knew that others were praying for him his confidence was strengthened even more, because Paul knew the truth of James 5:16, "The effective prayer of a righteous man can accomplish much."

*Confidence in the Provision of the Spirit.* Paul was certain that the Holy Spirit would grant him whatever was necessary to sustain him in any situation. The Greek word translated "provision" in Philippians 1:19 means "bountiful supply" or "full resources." Paul understood that he could rely on the complete resources of the Holy Spirit, based on what Jesus promised (Luke 11:13; John 14–16; Acts 1:8).

That truth is a source of confidence—not just for Paul, but also for us. Every genuine believer possesses the Holy Spirit and therefore has full access to His resources. Romans 8:26 says: "The Spirit also helps our weakness; for we do not know how to pray as we should, but the Spirit Himself intercedes for us with groanings too deep for words." That's how things work out for good (v. 28). Trials, tribulations, and sufferings don't resolve themselves for us in some vacuum. But we are able to endure them through the provision of God's Spirit—a provision we can know by faith and obedience.

*Confidence in the Promise of Christ.* Finally, Paul leaned on Jesus' promise to him when he was converted: "For this purpose I have appeared to you, to appoint you a minister and a witness" (Acts 26:16). Paul knew for certain that God had called him to a specific ministry, and as long as he was faithful he would never suffer shame (Mark 8:38).

Paul also expressed a simple trust in the words of Christ, the Good Shepherd, "My sheep hear My voice, and I know them, and they follow Me; and I give eternal life to them, and they shall never perish; and no one shall snatch them out of My hand" (John 10:27-28). Paul also would have known well the words of Moses from Deuteronomy 31:6, "Be strong and courageous, do not be afraid or tremble at them, for the Lord your God is the one who goes with you. He will not fail you or forsake you." The Lord never abandons His own, no matter how bleak our prospects in life, or how frustrating and fearful our circumstances.

In summarizing his attitude toward life and death, Paul says, "To me, to live is Christ, and to die is gain" (Phil. 1:21). To Paul, Christ was the reason for his existence. That's why his only real concern in life was serving Christ and proclaiming His Gospel. As long as he met that objective, Paul didn't care if he lived or died. In fact, given the choice, he would just as soon die, because dying is the ultimate gain for the believer. Death frees us from the burdens of this life and allows us to glorify Christ in eternity.

Paul was a man who stripped out of his life every single thing but Christ. Since Christ was his top priority, none of the opposition he confronted—prison, detractors, the threat of death—could deter him or shake his faith.

We can draw from the same words or precepts of God that Paul did. We can also ask other Christians to pray for us in times of great distress. We certainly have the same provision of the Holy Spirit as Paul did if we are genuine believers in Christ (Rom. 8:15-17). Finally, in the Gospels we can rely on the same promises of Christ that were available to Paul. Jesus has not changed and will not change (Heb. 13:8).

## KNOWING THE PARADOXES OF SUFFERING

Besides his opposition in Rome, Paul also suffered heavy criticism from detractors in the Corinthian church. They were false teachers bent on replacing Paul's teachings with their own lies. To gain the upper hand, those critics maligned Paul's person and character from all angles. They blamed him for being inept, ugly, blemished in appearance, unimaginative, a bad orator, and lacking in persona. Those particular attacks forced Paul into the delicate situation of needing to defend himself for the sake of God's truth without simultaneously being boastful or self-serving.

Paul solved that dilemma in a most remarkable and godly manner by agreeing with his detractors. He compared himself to a baked clay container (an earthen vessel or pot, which was often used as a garbage pail)—a metaphor for all the frailties and drawbacks his critics accused him of having. But at the same time he noted that this clay container had the treasure of God's truth in it. In taking this line of defense, Paul revealed his true humility in the face of adversity. He took the spotlight off himself and put it on Christ (2 Cor. 4:5) by contrasting his own weakness with the power of God's truth: "that the surpassing greatness of the power may be of God and not from ourselves" (v. 7).

However, in comparing himself to a clay pot, Paul does not want to be underestimated or misunderstood. He immediately lists a short series of paradoxes to show that his humility and human weakness does not cripple him in the midst of suffering: "We are afflicted in every way, but not crushed; perplexed, but not despairing; persecuted, but not forsaken; struck down, but not destroyed" (vv. 8-9). Paul continues to demonstrate that he is a man of contrasts—humble but invincible, aware of his weaknesses but gaining strength from them.

Each of these paradoxes involves conflict with an adversary. "Afflicted" means "pressure"—the extreme

pressure of potential death that Paul faced every day
from his foes. It was much more than the kind of daily
pressure and stress we all face as we do our jobs, minister to our families, or serve in our local churches. In one
notable instance Paul was stoned and actually left for
dead outside the city of Lystra (Acts 14:19-20). That
truly was a case of being near death, with seemingly no
escape, and emerging victorious.

The second paradox or contrast for Paul amid his
trials and sufferings is that he was "perplexed, but not
despairing." He sometimes wondered why he was constantly confronted with difficulties, but he always trusted God for a way out of each situation and therefore
never quit. Besides being a role model for handling
suffering, Paul was also a noble example of perseverance in the faith (Heb. 12:1-2).

Third, Paul says he was "persecuted, but not forsak-
en." The Greek word (dioko) that's translated "persecuted" has the more precise meaning of "pursue" or
"stalk," as when hunting an animal. This understanding of the usage here should dispel any notions we
might have that Paul suffered only routine, light persecution. He actually suffered much more frequent and
intense opposition than most of us could ever imagine.
Paul's tribulations were not such that anyone can claim
he overcame them by his own strength and willpower.
Only the power of God would do (2 Cor. 4:7), and
that power is also more than sufficient for us in the
difficulties we are likely to face (see Heb. 12:3).

Finally, Paul says he was "struck down, but not
destroyed." The Greek word translated "struck down"
literally means "to be struck with a weapon," whether
by a sword, spear, or an opponent's fist. The word was
also used in connection with ancient boxing and wres-

tling. Paul knew what it was like to be knocked down or slammed to the mat. At the same time, he also could testify that no blows were enough to destroy him or make him quit.

Paul's four paradoxes in the face of suffering give us additional reason to marvel at his testimony. They are also reminders that we do not realize power by avoiding suffering but by enduring it. Paul was completely committed to tenacious perseverance through any difficulty. Certainly he knew the truth and reality of the Prophet Isaiah's words concerning God's care for His own:

> But now, thus says the Lord, your creator, O Jacob, and He who formed you, O Israel, "Do not fear, for I have redeemed you; I have called you by name; you are Mine! When you pass through the waters, I will be with you; and through the rivers, they will not overflow you. When you walk through the fire, you will not be scorched, nor will the flame burn you. For I am the Lord your God, the Holy One of Israel, your Savior" (Isa. 43:1-3).

## ENDURANCE IN SUFFERING

Our study of Paul has revealed him to be a great model of one who victoriously endured sufferings, trials, and persecutions. He did so not only because he had to overcome the various obstacles to accomplish God's work, but there was a higher, overarching reason as well. Speaking of himself, Paul writes, "Therefore, since we have this ministry, as we received mercy, we do not lose heart" (2 Cor. 4:1).

"This ministry" refers to the privilege Paul had of ministering the truths of the New Covenant. After recounting the glorious features of the New Covenant in 2 Corinthians 3—the Holy Spirit, eternal life, the Resurrection, liberty in the Gospel of Christ, Paul could not and would not "lose heart" because of all the severe hardships he encountered. No amount of trouble could make Paul neglect his duty as a minister of the New Covenant, as the record of his life verifies.

The apostle again says "we do not lose heart" in 2 Corinthians 4:16-18, where he goes on to give three reasons that he endured suffering:

> Therefore we do not lose heart, but though our outer man is decaying, yet our inner man is being renewed day by day. For momentary, light affliction is producing for us an eternal weight of glory far beyond all comparison, while we look not at the things which are seen, but at the things which are not seen; for the things which are seen are temporal, but the things which are not seen are eternal.

Our modern culture has made it difficult for us to maintain an appreciation for the concept of endurance. Advances in science and technology have led us to expect shortcuts and quick fixes to avoid pain and inconvenience. One example of that is the overabundance and convenience of over-the-counter pain relievers. Advertisers claim that just by taking one or two pills, you should obtain fast relief from headaches, stuffy sinuses, and a variety of other physical aches and pains. There is seldom a willingness to slow down and learn to endure in a world of quick pain relief and creature comfort.

Paul's eternal perspective is clearly evident in verses 16-18. Each of his three reasons for endurance stress the value of what's lasting over what's fleeting. They are relevant for us whenever we struggle with a trial or suffering and become overwhelmed by the immediacy of the pain and circumstances.

### Endurance: Spiritual Is Greater than Physical

Paul was able to endure any physical suffering, first of all, because he was more concerned with what was happening in the spiritual realm than the physical. Paul accepted the fact that we live in physical bodies; his use of the term "earthen vessels" has already indicated that. But he also knew that our present bodies are decaying and therefore are not permanent. They are undergoing a natural aging process.

The Apostle Paul was perhaps more aware of this aging process than most. Because his lifestyle was full of rigorous ministry and travel demands, he aged more quickly. He was wearing out in service to God, much like Henry Martyn in India or David Brainerd among the American Indians in New England. Those servants of Christ both died before the age of thirty-five. Paul lived longer than they did (perhaps to age sixty), but nevertheless he was prematurely old and had worn himself out in the ministry.

Paul also aged quicker than normal because of the relentless abuse he suffered at the hands of his foes— an abuse that was physical and emotional. Even though he ultimately overcame all the persecution, it had to take its toll on his body.

In spite of that, Paul could say confidently that his inner man was being renewed daily (2 Cor. 4:16). In direct correlation to the decaying of his outer man (physical body) was the growth and maturing of his inner man, the nonmaterial, eternal side of us that is made into a new creation, what Ephesians 4:24 and Colossians 3:10 call the "new self." Paul was much more concerned about its renewal than about any decline in his physical side (see also Eph. 3:16).

Once again we must challenge ourselves to follow Paul's splendid example of endurance through life's variety of sufferings. It's not easy to imitate Paul and take our eyes off ourselves and our physical situations, yet we must do so, just as he exhorts us to "Set your mind on the things above, not on the things that are on earth" (Col. 3:2).

God often sends suffering our way to drive us to Him and compel us to look away from ourselves. We have all seen Him do so, if not in our lives then in the lives of others who have endured major trials or physical suffering and have grown in their faith as a result. Paul's consistent example is proof that suffering is directly related to spiritual growth. If his life is not proof enough, we can listen to the promises elsewhere in Scripture. Peter wrote, "After you have suffered for a little, the God of all grace, who called you to His eternal glory in Christ, will Himself perfect, confirm, strengthen and establish you" (1 Peter 5:10). Isaiah 40:28-31 says,

> Do you not know? Have you not heard? The Everlasting God, the Lord, the Creator of the ends of the earth does not become weary or tired. His understanding is inscrutable. He gives strength to the weary, and to him who lacks might He increases power. Though youths grow weary and tired, and vigorous young men

stumble badly, yet those who wait for the Lord
will gain new strength; they will mount up
with wings like eagles, they will run and not
get tired, they will walk and not become weary.

That key passage promises that the Lord will give us
the endurance we need as we look away from the
physical and toward the spiritual.

### Endurance: Value the Future over the Present

Paul's second secret for endurance through sufferings
and trials is valuing the future over the present. For
him it was a matter of looking beyond the present afflictions to realize that they are "producing for us an
eternal weight of glory far beyond all comparison"
(2 Cor. 4:17). The pain he was enduring on earth was
inconsequential compared to that great future reality
(Rom. 8:18).

The heavenly perspective Paul demonstrates is truly astounding. He characterizes his troubles as "momentary, light affliction" when all along we have noted
that his persecutions were heavy and constant. But
that's our earthly perspective. Paul viewed his difficulties as transitory as the vapor of life (see James 4:14)
and as light as fluff. The Greek *elaphros,* translated
"light" in 2 Corinthians 4:17, technically means
"weightless trifle," and that's what Paul's afflictions
were when considered from a heavenly standpoint.

In the first two chapters of this book we have affirmed that persecution is inevitable and suffering is
real; but when compared to what awaits us in the
future, they are, at their worst, light and trivial. The
true significance of suffering comes only when we see
how it contributes to our eternal glory. The Apostle

Peter again reinforces Paul's perspective: "In this you greatly rejoice, even though now for a little while, if necessary, you have been distressed by various trials, that the proof of your faith, being more precious than gold which is perishable, even though tested by fire, may be found to result in praise and glory and honor at the revelation of Jesus Christ" (1 Peter 1:6-7).

All our troubles and sufferings have a causal effect on our future glory. This effect is not meritorious but productive—it produces an eternal weight of glory. The Greek word (*barus*) translated "weight" more precisely means "heavy." It's as if Paul's sufferings were building up a heavy mass on one side of an old-fashioned scale. The mass represents the eternal weight of glory that is tipping the scale in favor of the future over the present. In essence Paul could tolerate the present pain as long as it had a positive impact on his future glory.

According to Scripture there is always a corresponding relationship between present suffering and future glory. Even Christ, as we shall see in greater detail in the next chapter, is an example of this principle. Philippians 2:8-9 says, "He humbled Himself by becoming obedient to the point of death, even death on a cross. Therefore also God highly exalted Him, and bestowed on Him the name which is above every name." The greater the suffering the greater the eternal reward. To the degree that we as believers suffer now, we will rejoice when we arrive in heaven because we will see the reward of our suffering (1 Peter 4:13). And that reward has nothing to do with sheer external bonuses (fancier crowns, larger heavenly dwelling places), but it relates to our increased capacity to praise, serve, rejoice, and glorify God. That was Paul's lifelong desire, and it should be ours as well.

### Endurance: Value the Eternal over the Temporal

The third way the Apostle Paul endured through many hardships and sufferings was by placing a greater value on eternal things than on temporal things: "We look not at the things which are seen, but at the things which are not seen; for the things which are seen are temporal, but the things which are not seen are eternal" (2 Cor. 4:18).

Paul's perspective on endurance through suffering—placing the spiritual and the future over the physical and the present—was not automatic. That is evident in the phrase, "while we look." The conditional force attached to it indicates that as long as our gaze is fixed, by faith, in the right place—looking at what is unseen—we will give the priority to future, spiritual realities and therefore endure with patience and grace the sufferings of this life.

I mention the element of faith parenthetically because it's implicit rather than explicit in Paul's statement. But that does not lessen the importance of faith as it relates to what is unseen. The author of Hebrews writes: "Now faith is the assurance of things hoped for, the conviction of things not seen. . . . By faith we understand that the worlds were prepared by the word of God, so that what is seen was not made out of things which are visible. . . . And without faith it is impossible to please Him, for he who comes to God must believe that He is, and that He is a rewarder of those who seek Him" (11:1, 3, 6). Faith is a basic component of the Christian life, and by its very definition we can see that God gives high priority to the invisible over the visible.

Since Paul recognized that priority, it should not be any different for contemporary Christians who want to be obedient, whether enjoying times of blessing and comfort or enduring times of difficulty and suffering. During his ministry, Paul was absorbed with the invisible, eternal world—a realm in which his greatest concerns were worshiping and glorifying God, serving Christ, and saving the souls of lost men and women. When we focus on the things of genuine lasting value—eternal things—temporal pains and difficulties, even the most severe, become much more bearable. But the key is our eternal perspective and priority, as the Lord Jesus instructs us in the Sermon on the Mount:

> Do not lay up for yourselves treasures upon earth, where moth and rust destroy, and where thieves break in and steal. But lay up for yourselves treasures in heaven, where neither moth nor rust destroys, and where thieves do not break in or steal; for where your treasure is, there will your heart be also (Matt. 6:19-21).

Paul remains a superb role model for how to deal with suffering. He did not rely on his own strength nor on some secret formula for successful living. Instead, his key to success was maintaining his focus on Christ's kingdom and the glory of God. To accomplish his vision, Paul confidently drew from God's complete supply of spiritual resources: His Word, His Spirit, His Son, and the prayers of fellow Christians. Paul could rejoice continually at these great provisions of grace, and so can we. That is not always easy, but true joy comes through Spirit-empowered perseverance to live the Christian life. Paul again gives us the pattern: "Do you not know that those who run in a race all run, but only one receives the prize? Run in such a way that you may win. And everyone who competes in the games exercises self-control in all things. They then do it to receive a perishable wreath, but we an imperishable" (1 Cor. 9:24-25). If we are already running to win the prize, there is no suffering, trial, or persecution that can discourage us or defeat us.

# FOUR

# *The Silence of the Lamb of God*

Arandom survey of various people in Western society concerning their ideas and images of Jesus would yield a variety of opinions about Him. Many would have a Christmas view of Him as a baby in a manger. Others would think of Him as an intelligent child who worked with His father in a Nazareth carpenter shop and on one occasion confounded the religious teachers in Jerusalem. Some survey respondents would see Jesus as a gentle, loving teacher who identified with the common people. Others would view Him as a compassionate but powerful healer who could cure all physical and emotional ailments and could even raise the dead. And there would be other answers, containing some degree of truth, supplying some legitimate piece of the picture of who Jesus was, yet incomplete.

But one image of Christ is the truest and most necessary perception of Him: the image that presents Him as the suffering Jesus, the crucified One. The Apostle

Paul summarizes well the believer's relationship toward this image: "For I determined to know nothing among you except Jesus Christ, and Him crucified" (1 Cor. 2:2). We cannot conclude our study of role models in suffering without this final chapter dealing with Jesus as the supreme example.

The Apostle Peter sets forth the issues for us quite well:

> For what credit is there if, when you sin and are harshly treated, you endure it with patience? But if when you do what is right and suffer for it you patiently endure it, this finds favor with God. For you have been called for this purpose, since Christ also suffered for you, leaving you an example for you to follow in His steps, who committed no sin, nor was any deceit found in His mouth; and while being reviled, He did not revile in return; while suffering, He uttered no threats, but kept entrusting Himself to Him who judges righteously (1 Peter 2:20-23).

According to Peter, Christians are at odds with the world, simply because they have been called by Christ. By standing with Christ, sooner or later we will suffer some form of unjust rejection, punishment, criticism, or persecution. We offend the world when we take a stand for righteousness or manifest a lifestyle that reflects Christ. That's why we have to expect suffering. Jesus Himself promised believers that their union with Him would elicit the hostility of the world:

> If the world hates you, you know that it has hated Me before it hated you. If you were of the

world, the world would love its own; but because you are not of the world, but I chose you
out of the world, therefore the world hates you.
Remember the word that I said to you, "A slave
is not greater than his master." If they persecuted Me, they will also persecute you; if they kept
My word, they will keep yours also. But all
these things they will do to you for My name's
sake, because they do not know the One who
sent Me (John 15:18-21).

But rest assured, God has not left us completely on
our own. Peter tells us in 1 Peter 2:21 that we have an
example in suffering: Christ Himself. He sets the standard, which is that the path to glory is the path of
suffering (Heb. 2:10; 5:8-9). And if we have such a pace-
setter in Jesus, it should not be difficult to realize the
truth of His words in Matthew 10:21-25,

And brother will deliver up brother to death,
and a father his child; and children will rise up
against parents, and cause them to be put to
death. And you will be hated by all on account
of My name, but it is the one who has endured
to the end who will be saved. But whenever
they persecute you in this city, flee to the next;
for truly I say to you, you shall not finish going
through the cities of Israel, until the Son of Man
comes. A disciple is not above his teacher, nor a
slave above his master. It is enough for the disciple that he become as his teacher, and the
slave as his master. If they have called the head
of the house Beelzebul, how much more the
members of his household!

## JESUS THE SINLESS SUFFERER

When experiencing a trial or enduring a time of suffering, many believers ask God these questions: Why has this happened? or What have I done wrong to deserve this? Those types of questions are usually formed at the beginning of a trial, long before a resolution is in sight. Those who are suffering, or those who seek to counsel the sufferers, are all too quick to name sin as the standard cause for the distress. It reminds me of the misconception the disciples had in John 9:2 concerning the man born blind, when they asked Jesus, "Rabbi, who sinned, this man or his parents, that he should be born blind?" Jesus corrected them immediately: "It was neither that this man sinned, nor his parents; but it was in order that the works of God might be displayed in him" (9:3). Similarly, Eliphaz, Bildad, and Zophar were wrong in their presumptuous and misguided assessments of their friend Job's plight (see Job 3–31). Job was not suffering because he had sinned (Job 1:1–2:11).

Our Lord Jesus Christ, in His own suffering and death, is an unequalled example of the reality that one can be completely in the will of God, supremely gifted and used by God in ministry, and perfectly righteous and obedient toward God, and still undergo tremendous suffering. Jesus was tried and executed as a criminal, yet He had done nothing wrong. He was the ultimate subject of unjust suffering and punishment, and He thereby gave us the standard for how to respond to our unjust persecution.

The very nature and circumstances of Christ's sufferings exposes as utterly false the present-day notion that Christians who suffer are always sinning or out of God's will. If Jesus, who was the perfect, sinless Son of God, suffered so much, then how can Christians who are so imperfect expect to escape all sufferings? The answer is that we cannot, as 1 Peter 2:20-23 demonstrates.

Such a theology of nonsuffering, if carried to its logical extreme, must claim that Jesus was out of God's will when He died on the cross. That thinking is more than bad logic, it is downright heretical.

Let's look more closely at 1 Peter 2:21 concerning the meaning of two Greek words and how the understanding of them will help us in our relationship to Christ and suffering. The second part of the verse says, "leaving you an *example* for you to follow in His *steps*" (emphasis mine).

The word "example" is the Greek word *hupogrammos*, which literally means "writing under." It carried with it the idea of a young child learning to write the alphabet by putting a model under the writing surface and tracing over the model. In the same way Christ is our model to trace as we anticipate suffering and how to handle it.

The word "steps" is the Greek *ichnos*, meaning "line of footprints" or "tracks." We are to follow in Jesus' tracks because the path to glory that He walked is the path of righteousness, and the path of righteousness in an unrighteous world is also a path of unjust suffering. If we want to be on the right path, we have to follow His footprints.

This idea parallels Paul's admonition, "All who desire to live godly in Christ Jesus will be persecuted" (2 Tim. 3:12). Not all Christians will suffer in the same manner or to the same degree, but those who seek to walk the path of righteousness that leads to glory will encounter trials, adversity, and suffering.

## JESUS THE HUMBLE SUFFERER

Through the eyes of the Prophet Isaiah, 1 Peter 2:22-23 gives us a closer look at Christ's manner of suffering. The Apostle Peter partially quotes the Septuagint (Greek Old Testament) version of Isaiah 53:9 to further describe Jesus' general reaction to unjust treatment. The first part of Peter's quote is actually a paraphrase that blends Isaiah's "violence" with the Septuagint's "lawlessness" to simply say "sin." The apostle, under the inspiration of the Holy Spirit, is simply stating what he knew the translators and Isaiah meant, namely that Jesus never violated God nor His law: He "committed no sin." Jesus reacted to the most difficult circumstances of unjust persecution with perfect dignity and humble composure.

To underscore his statement about sinlessness Peter quoted the last phrase of Isaiah 53:9, "nor was any deceit found in His mouth." The first and most readily apparent place that sin shows itself is the human mouth. Christ Himself had already taught that the heart speaks through the mouth: "But the things that proceed out of the mouth come from the heart, and those defile the man. For out of the heart come evil thoughts, murders, adulteries, fornications, thefts, false witness, slanders" (Matt. 15:18-19; see also 12:34-37).

Peter continues his thoughts from Isaiah 53 in 1 Peter 2:23. This time he draws from 53:7, which actually says, "He was oppressed and He was afflicted, yet He did not open His mouth; like a lamb that is led to slaughter, and like a sheep that is silent before its shearers, so He did not open His mouth." Thus, in somewhat of an irony, both Peter and Isaiah compare the suffering Christ, the Good Shepherd, to a sheep. It is common knowledge that sheep are not the most intelligent or self-sufficient creatures. The unabridged dictionary, in a secondary definition, refers to a person called a sheep as "one that is like a sheep (as in being a defenseless, innocent creature or in being readily preyed upon or shorn)."

That portrayal emphasizes the model our Lord displayed for endurance through suffering. He reveals His humility as He puts Himself at the mercy of His enemies. They reviled Him and provoked Him and abused Him repeatedly, nearly to the breaking point, but they couldn't make Him end His silence in a sinful way. Peter's statement "while being reviled" (1 Peter 2:23) refers to the repeated nature of the abuse hurled against Jesus. The fact that the original verb is in participle form here, indicating repeated action, serves to strengthen our previous comment. All the Gospel accounts of the Lord's sufferings underscore the silent humility with which He received so much verbal and physical abuse (see Matt. 26:57-63; Mark 15:3-5; Luke 23:9; John 19:9). Most of us can identify much easier with the Apostle Paul. Notice how he responded when Ananias the high priest commanded a soldier to strike him:

> Then Paul said to him, "God is going to strike you, you whitewashed wall! And do you sit to try me according to the Law, and in violation of the Law order me to be struck?" But the bystanders said, "Do you revile God's high priest?" And Paul said, "I was not aware, brethren, that he was high priest; for it is written, 'You shall not speak evil of a ruler of your people'" (Acts 23:3-5).

Contrary to our picture in chapter 3 of Paul as a role model in times of stress, here is an episode in which Paul failed. In this particular instance, Paul's sinful flesh got in the way, but that never occurred with Jesus. He is our perfect standard for how to control the tongue in the midst of unjust persecution and suffering, and to endure patiently for the joy that is to come (Heb. 12:2).

Jesus' silent humility is revealed in Peter's next quote from Isaiah 53: "He did not revile in return; while suffering, He uttered no threats" (1 Peter 2:23). In the face of an unbelievable amount of intense physical and verbal cruelty and assassination of perfect virtue, all of it unjustified, He did not retaliate. Since Jesus was God, He was able to exercise perfect control of His feelings and powers. He could have destroyed all His tormentors and instantly sent them to hell. But once again we see Jesus providing us the perfect example of how to behave in a time of unjust crisis and tribulation.

Christ's example of saying nothing and not answering in kind to unjust abuse seems like an impossible one to follow. But Peter shows us how Christ was able to achieve such a high standard: He "kept entrusting Himself to Him who judges righteously" (1 Peter 2:23). That's how Jesus found the strength to endure suffering, and that's how we are to do it as well.

"Entrusting" comes from *paradidomi*, which means "to hand over to someone to keep." Literally, Jesus kept handing Himself and the circumstance of every unjust suffering over to God. This pattern climaxed when Jesus was on the cross: "Jesus, crying out with a loud voice, said, 'Father, into Thy hands I commit My spirit.' And having said this, He breathed His last" (Luke 23:46).

Christ gave Himself over to God, even in death, because He knew that the Father would evaluate fairly all His unjust suffering (Gen. 18:25). Subsequently, when we are persecuted unjustly at our jobs, in our families, or in our social contacts, we need to follow His example and accept the persecution without retaliating. It is crucial that we resist by God's grace and power the urge to strike back or seek revenge in the midst of unjust persecution (Rom. 12:17-21). We simply need to entrust our souls continuously, by faith, to the care of the One who will pronounce a righteous verdict and who will bring us to eternal glory (John 15:5; 1 Peter 5:6-10).

In 1555, the English bishop, Reformer, and martyr Hugh Latimer was sentenced to be burned at the stake for his pro-Reformation positions. Prior to his death his convictions were set forth in an open letter to all genuine believers in Jesus Christ. This in part is what Latimer wrote: "Die once we must; how and where, we know not. . . . Here is not our home; let us therefore accordingly consider things, having always before our eyes that heavenly Jerusalem, and the way thereto in persecution" (cited in Harold S. Darby, *Hugh Latimer* [London: Epworth Press, 1953], 237). Latimer was executed later in 1555 along with his dear friend and colleague Nicholas Ridley. At that time, as the flames were being lit, an amazingly composed Latimer encouraged his fellow martyr with these words: "Be of good comfort, master Ridley, and play the man. We shall this day light such a candle, by God's grace, in England, as I trust shall never be put out" (Darby, 247). It is obvious that Hugh Latimer knew a lot about the power of suffering—far more than most Christians today—and he knew Jesus Christ and His standard for how to face unjust persecution and death.

In conclusion, it is clear that Jesus is not just the supreme and unequalled role model of suffering. Jesus is *the* example in everything. As our Lord and Savior, He is superior to the Old Testament prophets, which the writer of the letter to the Hebrews confirms at the very beginning of his book: "God, after He spoke long ago to the fathers in the prophets in many portions and in many ways, in these last days has spoken to us in His Son, whom He appointed heir of all things, through whom also He made the world" (1:1-2). Stephen and Paul were strong models of how believers can emerge victorious through any number of sufferings and persecutions, even the ultimate one of death. But these men were themselves simply "fixing [their] eyes on Jesus, the author and perfecter of faith" (Heb. 12:2), just as we need to do.

Only Christ was the sinless sufferer, with perfect reactions to everything He endured, thus qualifying Him to be the only model we need when going through trials, persecutions, sufferings, and temptations. The examples of other biblical role models can be instructive and inspirational, but only Jesus sits at the right hand of the Father as His Son and our intercessor (Heb. 4:14-16).

Paul counseled and encouraged Timothy about many things, but it all could perhaps be summarized in 2 Timothy 2:8: "Remember Jesus Christ, risen from the dead, descendant of David." He was exhorting Timothy to remember that Jesus in His humanity had already walked in the paths that we now walk. Whenever the going gets tough we can always come to Him in prayer, confident that He will fully empathize with what we are enduring. It is truly comforting to be able to talk to the One who has experienced it all and emerged successful every time. Other people may try to sympathize with our suffering, but they can never understand as Jesus can.

Christ is able to sympathize with us, His children, regarding the normal problems, pains, and struggles we encounter in life. But His sympathy certainly includes those significant times when our pain and suffering seem unbearable. If Jesus expresses loving concern for the smallest of our troubles, certainly in His role as the perfect sufferer He cares for our greatest traumas.

# FIVE

# *Preparing for Suffering*

**N**atural disasters are more frequent than ever — or so it seems. Many of us have vivid memories of the disasters that have occurred just since 1989, even if we were not directly affected by the events. An unprecedented rash of tragedies took place between late 1989 and early 1994: Hurricanes Hugo and Andrew in the southeastern United States, two major earthquakes in California, the blizzard of the century along the east coast in March 1993, extensive flooding in the Midwest in the summer of 1993, and damaging brush fires in Southern California in the fall of 1993. Then the world was surprised anew by the massive Japanese earthquake in January 1995.

All natural disasters are beyond the powers of men and women to predict or control with any precision. Certainly specific actions can lessen the impact of the calamity once it begins (sandbags for flood control, plowing during snowstorms), and a measure of general prediction exists so we can anticipate some events.

(Watches and warnings alert us to hurricanes, torna-
does, and snowstorms.) But it is generally conceded,
even by many secular scientists and commentators, that
natural disasters are unexpected "acts of God." The ex-
tent and severity of the suffering that results from most
disasters is also quite unanticipated. For instance, the
shock, stress, and hardship felt by victims of the
1989–94 catastrophes stretched the capacities of relief
agencies beyond the normal means needed to meet the
demands of victims.

Therefore, most natural upheavals are beyond our
control and in God's hands. Certain events, however,
can be anticipated and prepared for. (The city of St.
Louis escaped much of the damage of the 1993 Midwest floods because it had built a good system of sea-
walls in the wake of previous floods.) Likewise, in the
Christian life there will be unexpected storms of suffering, as well as hardships, that believers can prepare for.
In one of His parables, at the end of the Sermon on the
Mount, Jesus used a natural disaster comparison:

> Every one who hears these words of Mine, and
> acts upon them, may be compared to a wise
> man, who built his house upon the rock. And
> the rain descended, and the floods came, and
> the winds blew, and burst against that house;
> and yet it did not fall, for it had been founded
> upon the rock. And every one who hears these
> words of Mine, and does not act upon them,
> will be like a foolish man, who built his house
> upon the sand. And the rain descended, and
> the floods came, and the winds blew, and burst
> against that house; and it fell, and great was its
> fall (Matt. 7:24-27).

The key to preparedness in the Christian life is the foundation of truth upon which we build our lives—in other words, discipleship. If we are disobedient and refuse to walk loyally the narrow path of discipleship, sufferings, and trials will surprise and defeat us. So it is crucial for us to firmly grasp the role of the disciple. In that way we can guarantee our strength, endurance, and joy in suffering.

## SUFFERING COMES WITH DISCIPLESHIP

We have already looked at Jesus as the perfect example of how to face suffering. Since Jesus also sets the standard for discipleship, we need to consider our relationship to Him.

### *The Servant Is Not above His Teacher*
Jesus says in Matthew 10:24: "A disciple is not above his teacher, nor a slave above his master." That twofold statement is axiomatic; it doesn't have to be proved. In the first phrase we assume the disciple chooses his teacher, and in the second phrase we assume the master buys the slave or servant. Christ is simply saying that the first principle of discipleship is that we submit ourselves to Him. Our wills are prominent in the disciple/teacher relationship—we choose to learn under the direction of the teacher. Christ's sovereignty is prominent in the slave/master paradigm—He chooses us to be His servants. That is the basic duality inherent in the doctrine of salvation. In either case, it is obvious that we are to be submissive.

The relationship of disciple to teacher can be expressed positively in many ways as we seek to become Christlike (see Luke 6:40; Col. 3:16; 1 John 2:6). However, in the larger context of Matthew 10, Christ relates the truths of discipleship from a negative standpoint. The servant will not be exempt from persecution and opposition any more than Jesus was. This fact becomes clear as Jesus prepares the Twelve for ministry outreach and says they should expect hostility.

The same expectation applies to us. The more like Christ we become, the more the world will treat us as it treated Him. If we are not suffering much for His sake, then perhaps it's time to examine our lives (2 Cor. 13:5). If we want to be Christ's followers in every way, we need to be prepared to pay the price. In fact, Matthew 10:25 says, "It is enough for the disciple that he become as his teacher." That means we ought to be pursuing the goal of being like Jesus (cf. Phil. 3:14-17). We do not overstep our bounds in an effort to have greater privileges than Jesus had, nor do we look for ways to escape the demands and adversities He faced. When conformity to Him is as it should be, it becomes possible to triumph in suffering.

### The Servant Is Not Afraid of the World

As genuine followers of the Lord Jesus Christ, there is no reason to fear anything. Long before Christ came into the world, believers in God were encouraged not to fear: "The fear of man brings a snare, but he who trusts in the Lord will be exalted" (Prov. 29:25). The Apostle Paul exhorts Timothy along the same lines: "God has not given us a spirit of timidity [fear], but of power and love and discipline. Therefore do not be ashamed of the testimony of our Lord, or of me His prisoner; but join with me in suffering for the Gospel according to the power of God" (2 Tim. 1:7-8).

Fear is a powerful emotion that can weaken and

discourage us when facing any number of life's challenges. It certainly can operate in the realm of athletic competition. The poignant and inspiring story of American speed skater Dan Jansen during the last three Winter Olympics is a good illustration of how fear can inhibit performance. His odyssey began at the 1988 Winter Games in Calgary, Canada. There, as World Sprint Champion, he was favored to win a medal in either the 500-meter or 1,000-meter race, if not in both. Instead, he endured the heartbreak of falling during both races and not being able to finish either one. Because the races were held right after the death of his sister, Jansen's disappointing failures were attributed to the understandable emotional distress that anyone might feel at a time of family tragedy.

Dan Jansen's trail of frustration followed him to the next Winter Olympics in Albertville, France in 1992. He was expected to win at least one medal in speed skating, but again he failed in both the 500-meter and the 1,000-meter race. On those occasions he didn't fall, but here is how he described his effort in the 500-meters: "What happened was I skated a race that I can only describe as tentative. I looked good. I didn't slip. Yet something kept me from going flat out" (Dan Jansen with Jack McCallum, *Full Circle: An Olympic Champion Shares His Breakthrough Story* [New York: Villard Books, 1994]. Condensed in *Reader's Digest*, November 1994, 228). Implied in Dan's statement is an element of fear, perhaps stemming from his past failures, that kept him from going all-out in his competition. (His story finally had a happy ending at the 1994 Winter Olympics in Lillehammer, Norway, when he won the gold medal with a record-setting time in the 1,000-meters.)

The Christian life often parallels Dan Jansen's struggle with fear. Believers many times react fearfully when suffering or disappointment comes. Because so many Christians do not expect such trials and therefore are dealing with the unknown, the fear can be more painful and intense. But Jesus encouraged and exhorted His disciples at His Upper Room Discourse not to be afraid: "Peace I leave with you; My peace I give to you; not as the world gives, do I give to you. Let not your heart be troubled, nor let it be fearful" (John 14:27). This promise also is a powerful reassurance to us that the Spirit is always present, meaning we need not live under a cloud of fear.

In Matthew 10 Jesus gives us another strong antidote to the fear of suffering or persecution. He expresses what tremendous value God places on the life of every believer: "Are not two sparrows sold for a cent? And yet not one of them will fall to the ground apart from your Father. But the very hairs of your head are all numbered. Therefore do not fear; you are of more value than many sparrows" (vv. 29-31).

Jesus, according to His frequent practice, used an earthly illustration with commonplace objects to make His point. Here He uses small birds (sparrows), who were often eaten as hors d'oeuvres. His statement about the birds' falling to the ground implies precise knowledge and care by God toward His smallest creatures. In some Greek texts the word for "fall" is translated "hop." God not only knows when little birds die, but He knows when they hop—something they do all the time.

Jesus takes His illustration one step further by saying that God assigns a number to each one of the hairs on our heads (v. 30). Since it is estimated that the average human head has 140,000 hairs, God certainly knows each individual intimately.

The point of Jesus' illustration is simply this: If God takes care of little birds and assigns numbers to each hair of every person's head, certainly He is concerned about what happens to our minds, bodies, and eternal souls. He is concerned about our welfare and our ultimate good. No situation, no matter how bad or prolonged it may seem to us, is beyond God's ability to sustain us. Thus there is no room for debilitating fear (v. 31; see also 6:30-34).

### The Servant Is Prepared for the Worst

Preparedness is always the best policy, whether it be in the workplace, in governmental operations, or for anyone in his or her personal life. But sometimes people are insufficiently prepared for unexpected downturns in life. That was true regarding the bankruptcy of Orange County, California in December of 1994, a story that is still in the local media as I write this book.

Orange County, located just to the south of Los Angeles County, was one of the most prosperous areas in the United States, noted for its conservative politics and respected, upper middle-class communities. Now its reputation has suffered a huge blow due to the fiscal irresponsibility of some of its administrators. The county was forced to file for bankruptcy protection and had its assets frozen to prevent further investment losses (estimated to be 2 billion dollars). Suddenly the county found itself in the unenviable position of being the largest municipality in American history ever to declare bankruptcy.

In spite of behind-the-scenes warnings from investment experts that the financial situation in Orange County was precarious, there is little that could have prepared the average citizen of the county for such an unexpected shock. For some of them the impact was quite direct. School teachers, county workers, and small business owners who had contracts with the county were threatened with loss of paychecks. At this time it is not known what the long-term ill effects of the county's difficulties might be on individuals or on other counties and municipalities around the country.

The Orange County story provides this spiritual lesson: Never rule out the unexpected or the unprecedented negative event. Never say never to the possibility of a trial or painful season of suffering loss or disability. Facing such experiences is a part of the overall process in which we learn to follow the Lord more faithfully in every area of life (Josh. 24:15; Matt. 7:24-27; Rom. 12:1-2). The person who is already a disciple can also take comfort in the words of Isaiah: "The steadfast of mind Thou wilt keep in perfect peace, because he trusts in Thee. Trust in the Lord forever, for in God the Lord, we have an everlasting Rock" (26:3-4).

Dedicated, wholehearted followers of Christ will not be surprised by the worst of possible adversity or suffering, even if it takes the form of opposition from our own families:

> Do not think that I came to bring peace on the earth; I did not come to bring peace, but a sword. For I came to set a man against his father, and a daughter against her mother, and a daughter-in-law against her mother-in-law; and a man's enemies will be the members of his household. He who loves father or mother more than Me is not worthy of Me; and he who loves son or daughter more than Me is not worthy of Me (Matt. 10:34-37).

For those who are converted from an unbelieving family, persecution can be real and the struggles great. In those cases, the ones you love the most and with whom you should have the closest earthly relationships can often seem to be your worst enemies. Though the hatred may never result in execution, it often ends up in alienation.

Beyond that, Jesus sets forth an even greater challenge: "He who does not take his cross and follow after Me is not worthy of Me. He who has found his life shall lose it, and he who has lost his life for My sake shall find it" (vv. 38-39). Here Jesus stresses the need for total self-denial by His disciples, even if it meant their death.

My purpose in drawing us to Jesus' words about radical discipleship is to make clear that if our desire is to follow the Lord completely, then we need to be reminded of all that may be involved. If we are faithfully walking the path of discipleship daily, we will be aware of all the possible consequences of obedience.

When that's true, no circumstance of suffering will meet us as a total surprise. If we are called upon to suffer lengthy physical pain that may even conclude in death, we may be initially surprised. But if we are Christ's disciples, we won't remain in a state of shock. If God called the apostles and many others in the past to endure martyrdom, surely He has the right to send suffering to some of us—yet He is able to supply us with every resource we need to get through it (2 Cor. 12:7-10; Phil. 4:11-13; 1 Peter 5:6-7).

## DISCIPLESHIP DEFLECTS SUFFERING

The concept of preventive medicine has made moderate advances in recent years. For some people the best medicine is no medicine—they strive to stay in good shape to avoid illness and injury. The fitness craze and accompanying increased awareness of good eating habits are manifestations of this objective.

The idea of prevention has been around much longer in the realm of automotive maintenance. Many car owners faithfully change their motor oil every 3,000 miles and regularly keep an eye on other vital fluids, as well as the basic operating components of the car. These people would prefer to pay small amounts at regular intervals to have their cars well maintained, rather than risk an inconvenient breakdown or expensive major repair later.

We can apply that same prevention analogy to our Christian lives and particularly to our experiences with suffering. Preventative spiritual maintenance is implicit in being prepared for the unexpected and having a mind-set that accepts the basics of discipleship before sufferings and hardships happen. This kind of spiritual discipline allows us to react scripturally to trials and persecutions and appreciate their refining effects.

### Disciples React with Grateful Prayer
In Philippians 4:6 the Apostle Paul urges us to "be anxious for nothing, but in everything by prayer and supplication with thanksgiving let your requests be made known to God." This attitude of the mature and stable Christian—thankfulness in the face of any kind of problem—is a strong antidote to worry and anxiety. While it is assumed that we will cry out to God for help when problems come, Paul does not expect us to doubt, blame, or question God. That kind of attitude belies a dissatisfaction and discontent with His plan for us.

The true disciple reacts to suffering with an attitude

of thanksgiving because, as we have seen earlier, he knows God's promises and realizes that He has pledged that nothing will come into his life that he is unable to bear. God's ultimate goal is our perfection (1 Peter 5:10). We can be thankful because God has a purpose for us and He supplies us with His power so that we might cope triumphantly through the suffering.

Notice what Philippians 4:7 says about the results of such gratitude of heart: "The peace of God, which surpasses all comprehension, shall guard your hearts and your minds in Christ Jesus." All believers would like to know peace, tranquility, inner calm, and contentment while in the midst of difficult suffering. Verse 7 promises exactly such peace.

A prayerful attitude of thankfulness, no matter what the situation, results in our receiving the unsurpassed peace of God. Furthermore, a closer look at verses 6 and 7 reveals that what's at stake in the midst of our prayer is not God's specific answer, but the peace He provides. Therefore, whenever we are undergoing pain and suffering, we need to be clear that God is primarily concerned about our heart attitude, not with providing instant answers or relief according to our whims or desires. This truth does not originate with Paul but goes back to the earliest Old Testament days. The Book of Job is a good example, especially near the end of the book where God asks Job a long series of questions about Himself (Job 38–41). God did not answer the questions because that was not His purpose. He simply wanted Job to recognize and submit to His sovereignty.

Peace, when understood scripturally, is a marvelous concept. Here is what Bible scholar and my former teacher Dr. C.L. Feinberg says:

The primary and basic idea of the biblical word "peace" (OT *salom;* NT *eirene*) is completeness, soundness, wholeness. . . . The innumerable blessings of the Christian revolve around the concept of peace. The gospel is the gospel of peace (Eph. 6:15). Christ is our peace (Eph. 2:14-15); God the Father is the God of peace (1 Thes. 5:23). The inalienable privilege of every Christian is the peace of God (Phil. 4:9) because of the legacy of peace left by Christ in his death (John 14:27; 16:33). These blessings are not benefits laid up in glory only, but are a present possession (Rom. 8:6; Col. 3:15). Thus, peace is "a conception distinctly peculiar to Christianity, the tranquil state of a soul assured of its salvation through Christ, and so fearing nothing from God and content with its earthly lot, of whatever sort that is" (Thayer) ("Peace," in *Evangelical Dictionary of Theology,* edited by Walter A. Elwell [Grand Rapids: Baker, 1984], 833).

No matter how difficult your suffering, if you are sensitive to Philippians 4:7, God will grant you peace.

### Disciples Are Confident in God's Providence
In chapter 1 we affirmed the necessity of having a basic grasp of God's sovereignty in relation to sufferings and trials. In connection with our study of preparedness for adversity, we need to examine the facet of God's sovereignty known as providence.

Providence is a term not used in Scripture, but one that definitely denotes a biblical, doctrinal truth. (This phenomenon, of course, is not unique. Most of us are aware that the word *trinity* is not actually in the Bible.

But we know that the truth of this concept is implicit in Scripture and is a foundational Christian doctrine.) Providence is related to the idea that God provides and orchestrates everything through ordinary means and natural processes to accomplish His purpose.

Providence is the most frequent way that God operates in the world and controls the daily course of events to effect His purpose. The other way He can act in human society is by miracle, which He did numerous times during various periods of Bible history. (Although I believe God continuously operates at a supernatural level and anything is possible with Him, I do not believe He performs miracles today in the same way He did during the times of the prophets, Christ, and the apostles. For an elaboration of that view, see my book *Charismatic Chaos* [Grand Rapids: Zondervan, 1992], 106–27.) Whereas God operates providentially within the flow of history by bringing together all the numberless factors of the world of beings and events and coordinating them to achieve His purposes, miracles interrupted the flow of history and suspended one or more natural laws so He could supernaturally accomplish His will. It seems to me that believing in God's providence is a greater exercise of faith than is believing in comparatively uncomplicated miracles.

Ironically, however, some professing believers claim to have great faith in miracles, which have always been rare or even absent, and virtually demand God perform one to heal an injury, cure a disease, or deliver them from some crisis. But at the same time such people have little or no grasp of the truth of God's providence. In many ways the daily outworking of providence, in which God constantly must orchestrate millions of details and circumstances, is a greater miracle than what we ordinarily think of as a miracle. Faith in God's providence, therefore, contributes much to our overall contentment before God.

Paul had a genuine confidence in God's providence, whether things were easy or hard: "Not that I speak from want; for I have learned to be content in whatever circumstances I am" (Phil. 4:11). The patriarch Joseph acquired similar confidence through his experiences in Egypt. He summarizes so well to his brothers his faith in God's providence:

> Joseph said to them, "Do not be afraid, for am I in God's place? And as for you, you meant evil against me, but God meant it for good in order to bring about this present result, to preserve many people alive. So therefore, do not be afraid; I will provide for you and your little ones." So he comforted them and spoke kindly to them (Gen. 50:19-21).

You will never know all the benefits of the power of suffering until you realize that a sovereign God is providentially ordering everything for your good and His glory. Once you come to accept that God is in control of all things, you will be that much better prepared to deal with whatever hardships and sufferings He may choose to send your way—"We know that God causes all things to work together for good to those who love God, to those who are called according to His purpose" (Rom. 8:28).

### Disciples Are Prepared for Satan's Attacks

In considering spiritual preparedness in the face of potential suffering, there is the constant need to maintain a balance. This is especially important as we examine, even briefly, Satan's role in a believer's suffering. First Peter 5:8-9 says, "Be of sober spirit, be on the alert. Your adversary, the devil, prowls about like a roaring lion, seeking someone to devour. But resist him, firm in your faith, knowing that the same experiences of suffering are being accomplished by your brethren who are in the world." These verses suggest a very straightforward approach to dealing with Satan—in contrast to the extremes that would either deny the existence of a personal devil and demons (represented by atheists and secularists) or see him involved with and directly to blame for every single trouble a Christian will have (represented by evangelicals of various persuasions who encourage esoteric, nonstop spiritual warfare).

First, Peter's direct approach tells us to be alert. We must watch our surroundings and our relationships and be alert to potential temptations. In doing so we also must realize that Satan has already been defeated by Christ and that we, as believers, can see him defeated in our lives as well (1 John 4:4).

Second, Peter says we must "resist him [the devil], firm in [our] faith" (1 Peter 5:9). This admonition is very similar to the one James provides: "Resist the devil and he will flee from you" (4:7). "Resist" simply means "to stand up against." We do that by standing firm in the objective truth of our Christian faith and in our trust in God. Satan is a liar and deceiver, and meeting his attacks squarely with God's revealed truth is the most formidable and effective way to counter him.

Such a strategy is a far cry from what the spiritual warfare extremists believe. They claim we need to bind Satan, but it is not clear exactly what they mean by that. Scripture knows nothing of the contemporary view that believers can confront and "bind" Satan and his demons. If that were true, Peter, Paul, or one of the other New Testament writers would have affirmed such a ministry and provided some instruction regarding it. (For a fuller discussion of spiritual warfare, see my book *How to Meet the Enemy* [Wheaton, Ill.: Victor, 1992], especially chaps. 2–3.)

Scripture does confirm that Satan can have a role in suffering and persecution (Job 1:1–2:8; Matt. 4:1-11; Mark 1:21-27; 5:1-20). But in all those accounts God is in control. If any binding is to be done, Christ will send an angel to do it (see Rev. 20:1-3). Therefore, our duty now is to heed the instruction of Peter and James and remember that our vigilance against Satan is not accomplished in our own strength or by clever mental and verbal strategies. The Apostle Paul says,

> For though we walk in the flesh, we do not war according to the flesh, for the weapons of our warfare are not of the flesh, but divinely powerful for the destruction of fortresses. We are destroying speculations and every lofty thing raised up against the knowledge of God, and we are taking every thought captive to the obedience of Christ (2 Cor. 10:3-5).

The key to real preparedness for and awareness of Satan's role in suffering is to have our hearts and minds fixed on obedience to Christ and the truth. That's when we will be best prepared to benefit from the power of suffering when God sends trials, persecutions, and afflictions into our lives. A faithful disciple of the Lord is prepared for whatever comes.

# SIX

# *Dealing with Suffering*

Consider this quotation, which opens one of the closing chapters of a contemporary book on how to study the Bible:

> Many Christians are like poor photographs—overexposed and underdeveloped. They've had plenty of input from the Word of God, but what difference has it made in their lives? Spiritual growth is a commitment to change. And yet, the human heart resists nothing as strongly as it resists change. We will do anything to avoid it (Howard G. Hendricks and William D. Hendricks, *Living by the Book* [Chicago: Moody, 1991], 292).

Those observations were made in reference to applying the truths of Scripture. Application is the logical, final step in the Bible study process, but it is often mishandled or omitted altogether. As we near the conclusion of our study of suffering, I hope you'll not neglect or avoid applying what you have learned. With a difficult topic such as this one, it is especially important to ponder the issues that have an impact on your life. The primary question you need to ask yourself as you think about the possibility of facing trials and persecutions is "How will I react?" Either you will react with a positive attitude, like the men we studied in chapters 2–4, and enjoy positive benefits, or you will react negatively and compound the trouble.

## ATTITUDE CHECK:
## DEALING WELL WITH SUFFERING

We hear a lot today in the slang of popular culture about attitudes, and much of it is negative. The mere usage of the word *attitude*, as in "He really has an attitude," informs anyone who knows contemporary speech that the person we're describing has a bad or even surly attitude. Similarly, if someone needs an "attitude check," that means they need to exchange their negative demeanor for a positive attitude in the midst of a challenging situation.

The Apostle Peter's first letter focuses on the theme of suffering, and in it he presents two of the four elements that constitute a proper attitude in response to suffering:

> Beloved, do not be surprised at the fiery ordeal among you, which comes upon you for your testing, as though some strange thing were happening to you; but to the degree that you share the sufferings of Christ, keep on rejoicing; so that also at the revelation of His glory, you may rejoice

with exultation. If you are reviled for the name of
Christ, you are blessed, because the Spirit of glory
and of God rests upon you (4:12-14).

## DO NOT BE SURPRISED BY SUFFERING

The first attitudinal component that will help you
through the tough ordeals is to expect them. Inasmuch
as we are born to trouble as fallen sinners in a fallen
world of sinners, it is reasonable *not to be surprised* when
trouble shows up. In the context of this epistle, though
Peter is referring more precisely to persecution and its
inevitability, it still makes the point—expect trials.

Peter is echoing the instruction regarding suffering
by persecution that we find elsewhere in the New Testament (John 15–16; 2 Tim. 3:12; 1 John 3:13). The
words and actions of believers testify against an ungodly world. That should be expected to result in a back-
lash of persecution from unappreciative and offended
unbelievers, although it doesn't always happen. But
such a reaction toward us is part of the cost of discipleship, as we have already discussed.

Though his focus is on the persecution that comes
because of our faith in and identification with Jesus
Christ, Peter's use of the expression "fiery ordeal" in
1 Peter 4:12 could refer to any type of trouble. In both
the New Testament and the Greek Old Testament, the
word translated "fiery" is used for a furnace. In the Old
Testament it referred to a smelting furnace in which metal was melted down to be purged of foreign elements.
Psalm 66:10 says, "For Thou hast tried us, O God; Thou
hast refined us as silver is refined." Here in 1 Peter, therefore, fiery ordeal is symbolic of the affliction that God
designs "for your testing"—for your purification.

First Peter 4:12 concludes with the indication that
trials and persecutions are not "some strange thing"
that is out of the ordinary. Paul says all trials are "common to man" (1 Cor. 10:13). In essence Peter is saying
we should not be surprised by sufferings, as if they
were happening to us merely by chance. Persecution,
affliction, and suffering are part of life to be anticipated
and do not interfere with God's plan. They are common to all, and especially to obedient and faithful believers.

## REJOICE IN SUFFERING

The second positive element Peter wants us to have in
our attitude toward sufferings is *to rejoice in them.* This
calls to mind the words of the Lord Jesus in the Beati-
tudes, "Blessed are you when men revile you, and persecute you, and say all kinds of evil against you falsely,
on account of Me. Rejoice, and be glad, for your reward
in heaven is great" (Matt. 5:11-12). This is one of the
most challenging exhortations in Scripture. And Peter
affirms that the words are right when he says to "keep
on rejoicing" (continuous action) in 1 Peter 4:13. We
also saw in chapter 3 that the Apostle Paul demonstrated joy in the face of sufferings. This attitude is definitely present throughout Scripture and hard to avoid if we
want to be diligent to all that the Holy Spirit says. And
it makes sense to be joyful because of God's gracious,
sovereign providence and purpose in our suffering.
Even the worst suffering is working for our good (Rom.
8:28).

The gifted expositor D. Martyn Lloyd-Jones helps
us to distinguish carefully what is meant by the concept
of rejoicing in suffering:

Why is the Christian to rejoice like this [when facing persecution], and how is it possible for him to do so? Here we come to the heart of the matter. Obviously the Christian is not to rejoice at the mere fact of persecution. That is always something which is to be regretted. Yet you will find as you read Christian biographies that certain saints have faced that temptation very definitely. They have rejoiced wrongly in their persecution for its own sake. Now that, surely, was the spirit of the Pharisees, and is something which we should never do. If we rejoice in the persecution in and of itself, if we say, "Ah, well; I rejoice and am exceeding glad that I am so much better than those other people, and that is why they are persecuting me," immediately we become Pharisees. Persecution is something that the Christian should always regret; it should be to him a source of great grief that men and women, because of sin, and because they are so dominated by Satan, should behave in such an inhuman and devilish manner. The Christian is, in a sense, one who must feel his heart breaking at the effect of sin in others that makes them do this. So he never rejoices in the fact of persecution as such (*Studies in the Sermon on the Mount,* Vol. 1 of 2 vols. [Grand Rapids: Eerdmans, 1959], 142–43).

Therefore we must be clear that our text from 1 Peter is not saying (nor are other passages) that believers should have an elitist or masochistic attitude regarding suffering.

Our rejoicing is not to be connected with the pain or difficulty itself, but with the ramifications of it. Peter refers to some of those in 1 Peter 4:13.

The phrase "but to the degree that you share the sufferings of Christ" means that we are privileged, when persecuted for righteousness, to enjoy the fellowship of our Lord's suffering. That does not mean that we share the atoning sufferings of Christ. Rather, Peter is simply saying that believers can share in the same kind of suffering that Jesus endured and for His sake— suffering for proclaiming His saving Gospel. Paul was an example of one who suffered like that and he testified to it several times in his letters (Gal. 6:17; Phil. 1:29-30; 3:10; Col. 1:24). The other apostles learned quickly how to rejoice after suffering for Jesus' sake. For them such suffering was a tremendous privilege (Acts 5:40-41), and it can be for us also, if we approach it and receive it with the right attitude.

Peter continues in 4:13 to give us even more incentive to rejoice when suffering comes: "So that also at the revelation of His glory, you may rejoice with exultation." "The revelation of His glory" is simply another way of referring to Jesus' second coming (see Matt. 25:31; Luke 17:30). And "rejoice with exultation" gives more intensity to Peter's earlier usage of rejoice. If Christians are faithful to accept suffering and persecution as Christ did, then when He returns they will really rejoice, with an outburst that surpasses all other joys (see also Luke 6:22-23).

There is one additional reason for us to respond with an attitude of joy when we face persecution: the Holy Spirit rests upon us (1 Peter 4:14). At first glance that seems like such a simple statement of truth. But Peter's words, inspired by the very same Spirit he is speaking of, are truly awesome and profound. First, the Spirit's presence is not related to some vague, subjective feeling of blessing, typified by such exclamations as "This is such a blessing!" or "May the Lord bless you." Instead, His presence is objective—we can be sure He is there when we suffer or are persecuted.

The people of God through history have been very much aware of this reality. Peter calls the Holy Spirit "the Spirit of glory," which emphasizes that God, the third member of the Trinity, has glory as an essential attribute, as was revealed in the Shekinah light appearing in the Old Testament. It signified the presence of God, exemplified by the burning bush, the glow on the mountain, the pillar of fire that led the Israelites in the desert, and the cloud that entered the tabernacle and temple.

Although the Spirit does not display Himself in that way today, His glorious presence is nonetheless real for a believer who is in the center of suffering and persecution. This must mean something more than that which is normal for believers—namely, the indwelling of the Spirit. That is true of all believers all the time (Rom. 8:9). This resting of the Spirit on the suffering Christian is a special grace of ministry beyond the regular. As we studied in chapter 2, the Spirit of glory definitely rested on Stephen at the time of his stoning. The Holy Spirit refreshed him by taking over and becoming the dominant power to lift him above the agony (read again Acts 6–7).

The helpful truths of 1 Peter 4:13-14 provide vital reasons for us to engage attitudes of rejoicing in the middle of persecution and suffering. Throughout the centuries of church history, many saints who endured persecution and martyrdom have known the realities of the Apostle Peter's words. Thomas Cranmer (1489–1556; first Protestant Archbishop of Canterbury; author of the First and Second Prayer Books and the Thirty-nine Articles of the Church of England) followed in the path of Stephen and experienced the overcoming grace and strength of the Holy Spirit at the hour of his greatest crisis. He was arrested by the Roman Catholic Queen Mary in 1553 and was eventually burned at the stake because he would not renounce his Protestant beliefs. Here's how he dealt with his final suffering:

> Soon an iron chain was brought, and put around Cranmer, fastening him to the stake. Then when the fagots had been piled up the sheriff ordered fire to be brought. And when the wood was kindled, and the fire began to burn near him, he was seen by all who stood there, to stretch forth his right hand ... and to hold it in the flames. There he held it so unflinchingly that all the people saw it burned, before his body was touched by the fire. So patient and steadfast was he in the midst of this extreme torment, that he uttered no cry, and seemed to move no more than the stake to which he was bound. His eyes were lifted up to heaven, and he often repeated, "This was the hand that wrote it [a previous disavowal of Protestantism, an action he had since reversed]," — "this unworthy right hand," so long as his voice would suffer him; and as often using the words of the martyred St. Stephen, "Lord Jesus, receive my spirit!" till the fury of the flames putting him to silence, he gave up the ghost (John Foxe, *Foxe's Christian Martyrs of the World* [Chicago: Moody, n.d.], 506).

The only explanation we can give for Bishop Cranmer's amazing composure and fortitude in suffering was that the Spirit of glory rested upon him and spiritually lifted him above the physical pain and human fear. The same Spirit is abundantly available to us, allowing us to know the power of suffering in any persecution, tribulation, or trial we may have to endure. He gives grace that is unique to the requirements of our suffering.

## EVALUATING SUFFERING

Two other necessary elements to a right attitude in dealing with suffering are found in 1 Peter 4:15-19. Peter writes,

> By no means let any of you suffer as a murderer, or thief, or evildoer, or a troublesome meddler; but if anyone suffers as a Christian, let him not feel ashamed, but in that name let him glorify God. For it is time for judgment to begin with the household of God; and if it begins with us first, what will be the outcome for those who do not obey the gospel of God? And if it is with difficulty that the righteous is saved, what will become of the godless man and the sinner? Therefore, let those also who suffer according to the will of God entrust their souls to a faithful Creator in doing what is right.

The third feature we need in order to compose our response in dealing with suffering is *to evaluate it*. Asking God for the discernment to understand the suffering's purpose and how it contributes to placing us in the center of His will is something we ought not overlook.

Just to make sure no one is confused into thinking *all* suffering is God's will for believers, 1 Peter 4:15 mentions four evils for which we should never suffer. The first three—murder, theft, evildoing—are quite obvious and straightforward. The fourth one, "troublesome meddler," while at first glance appearing to be rather obvious, requires closer scrutiny to fully understand it in relation to our theme.

A troublesome meddler describes the person who is always interested in everyone's business but his own. Paul refers to this type of activity several times in his letters and says we should shun such intrusive behavior (1 Thes. 4:11; 2 Thes. 3:11; 1 Tim. 5:13). In those verses it is quite clear that meddling is evil behavior. But we can also look at the term from another angle and clear away some misconceptions regarding appropriate social action by Christians.

Some interpreters believe, and I agree, that 1 Peter 4:15 is referring to political agitation—revolutionary activity that seeks to disrupt and interfere with the function and flow of the existing government. If such an interpretation is accurate, then Peter is calling for Christians to live as good citizens in non-Christian cultures. This is consistent with what he wrote in 1 Peter 2:11-19 and what Paul called for in Romans 13:1-7 and Titus 3:1-4. They should do their jobs, live peaceable lives, share the Gospel, and exalt Christ. He leaves no room for believers to become revolutionaries in attempting to overturn the government or impose Christian standards on the culture or in the workplace. Being persecuted (or prosecuted) by the government because of troublesome agitation, or receiving discipline by an employer for disruptive activities, is not suffering for the right reason. It is not honorable as a Christian to be in that position—it is disgraceful.

A relevant and current example of this kind of meddlesome activity that requires punishment, yet is seen by some professing Christians as legitimate ministry, is the extreme protest strategy of some antiabortion groups. What I am referring to are acts of civil disobedience (blocking driveways of abortion clinics and refusing to comply with orders from the police), bombings of clinics, and killings of clinic workers and doctors. The murders and attempted murders of abortion personnel are the most heinous examples of such activism. Since early 1993, at least three such cases have been prominent in the news. One resulted in the 1994 conviction of a former Presbyterian minister, who glibly told reporters that he knew without a doubt that, should he be executed, he would go directly to heaven afterward.

Lest I be misunderstood, I want to affirm that I am unalterably opposed to the killing of unborn children. The Bible is quite clear in many references that God is concerned for the sanctity of life at all phases (Gen. 1:27; Ex. 21:22-25; Deut. 30:19; Job 10:8-12; 31:15; Pss. 100:3; 139:13-16; Matt. 18:6, 14; Gal. 1:15). I am also very aware that many dedicated and godly Christians are involved in the pro-life movement, and they have done much good work in the last twenty years to educate people on the importance of this cause. These pro-life workers have also helped provide beneficial counseling and material assistance through a variety of crisis pregnancy service agencies.

Therefore, I am not criticizing the legitimate, valid, peaceful efforts of the pro-life, antiabortion movement. I am merely pointing out that extremist actions, performed under the guise of Christianity, are wrong. Even implicit support by believers "from the sidelines" for such actions is not biblical. Any Christian involved in activities designed to promote what is right and redress what is unjust must use scriptural discernment to decide what strategies to support. To do otherwise is to become a "troublesome meddler," one who is not suffering for righteousness' sake.

The Apostle Peter presents one final reason for believers to evaluate suffering when it comes: "For it is time for judgment to begin with the household of God; and if it begins with us first, what will be the outcome for those who do not obey the Gospel of God?" (1 Peter 4:17) We must be prepared for sufferings because God is chastening, testing, and purifying us as members of His church at the end of the age. In verse 7 Peter indicates that we are now living in the end times: "The end of all things is at hand." Christ appeared at the beginning of this last era to suffer, die, and judge our sins on the cross. Our sufferings began at the cross and are part of God's unfolding plan that culminates with the Great White Throne. ("Time" in v. 17 more precisely means "season." It refers to the crucial moment or point in the history of God's revelation when judgment begins.)

The "household of God" (the church) is always in the process of being purged and purified. That has occurred throughout church history, from the first days of the church (Ananias and Sapphira; Acts 5), to the time of Peter's writing (under Nero and other Roman emperors), to Reformation times, right down to the twentieth century (in Eastern Europe and China). The process has not stopped, so we need to evaluate our own persecutions within the larger context of God's refining and purifying work in His church. There may be times when God needs to discipline us so that we may serve Him with greater effectiveness (Heb. 12:5-13).

Peter knew God's order of judgment in this age, that it begins with us and eventually falls upon unbelievers in full and final fury (far different from the refining and chastening that we experience). Peter uses that contrast to give us the right perspective on the whole process (1 Peter 4:17-18; see also 2 Thes. 1:4-7). Far better to endure some suffering as chastening for sin now while the Lord purges the church than to endure in the future the eternal sufferings of the unsaved.

## TRUSTING GOD IN SUFFERING

The fourth and final element the Christian sufferer should embrace in his attitude is that of *entrusting himself to God*. Peter writes: "Therefore, let those also who suffer according to the will of God entrust their souls to a faithful Creator in doing what is right" (1 Peter 4:19).

The word "entrust" is a banking term that means "to deposit for safekeeping." Peter is exhorting any believers who suffer to give their souls (lives) over to the care of God. Here Peter describes God as a "faithful Creator," which reminds us that He created us and is completely capable and trustworthy in taking care of all our needs.

The apostle is assuming that his audience, having just read the preceding verses (and many having personally experienced persecution), had a basic grasp of what suffering entails. So he presents God not only as the One who is faithful but also as the One who is sovereign. He has allowed suffering in their lives according to His overall plan and purpose. Therefore it is only logical and reasonable that Peter's readers be urged to trust God through trials and persecutions. It is only reasonable that we also should maintain an attitude of trust as we endure suffering. That is similar in principle to Paul's well-known exhortation in Romans 12:1, "I urge you therefore, brethren, by the mercies of God, to present your bodies a living and holy sacrifice, acceptable to God, which is your spiritual [or, rational] service of worship." Paul's words remind us again of the close connection between discipleship and suffering. It is so much easier to deal with suffering if we have already purposed in our hearts to turn everything over to the Lord. If we have an attitude of submission, obedience, and sacrificial service, we will not be concerned about the trials and persecution He may allow.

Jerry Bridges offers this additional insight regarding the challenge of trusting in God during times of suffering:

> To trust God in times of adversity is admittedly a hard thing to do. . . . Trusting God is a matter of faith, and faith is the fruit of the Spirit (Galatians 5:22). Only the Holy Spirit can make His Word come alive in our hearts and create faith, but we can choose to look to Him to do that, or we can choose to be ruled by our feelings of anxiety or resentment or grief.

John Newton, author of the hymn "Amazing Grace," watched cancer slowly and painfully kill his wife over a period of many months. In recounting those days, John Newton said:

> I believe it was about two or three months before her death, when I was walking up and down the room, offering disjointed prayers from a heart torn with distress, that a thought

suddenly struck me, with unusual force, to this effect—"The promises of God must be true; surely the Lord will help me, *if I am willing to be helped!*" It occurred to me, that we are often led . . . [from an undue regard of our feelings], to indulge that unprofitable grief which both our duty and our peace require us to resist to the utmost of our power. I instantly said aloud, "Lord, I am helpless indeed, in myself, but I hope I am willing, without reserve, that thou shouldest help me." (*Trusting God* [Colorado Springs: Navpress, 1988], 195–96. Newton quotation from John Newton, *The Works of John Newton* [reprint; Edinburgh: Banner of Truth, 1985], 5:621–22; emphasis in original.)

Geoffrey Bull is a modern example of one who entrusted his soul to God in severe suffering. Bull was imprisoned for more than three years by the Chinese Communists and subjected to solitary confinement, starvation, intimidation, and brainwashing. He wrote a poem in the midst of his ordeal, which asked that the Lord not allow the memory of His Word to grow dim nor let him succumb to doubt, loneliness, or fear. He further asked that God let him retain His peace and give him victory over fatigue.

The closing two lines of the poem expressed Bull's trust in the ultimate outworking of God's plan and purpose:

And Thy kingdom Gracious God,
Shall never pass away.
(cited by Paul S. Reese, *Triumphant in Trouble* [Westwood, N.J.: Revell, 1962], 119–20).

# SEVEN

# *The Lessons from Suffering*

A sign on the wall of a junior high classroom contained these words: "Experience is the hardest teacher. It gives the test first and then the lesson." This truism was likely forgotten by most of the students who used that classroom. Likewise, many Christians do not realize or forget that the experiences of the Christian life, whether difficult or pleasant, tend to be followed by an understanding of the lessons they are intended to teach us. In this final chapter we'll examine the general principles you can apply to your specific circumstances to begin to understand the lessons of suffering.

Not only does the Lord want us to be aware of truths and results that occur after periods of trial and suffering, He wants us to embrace the lessons as positives in the ongoing spirit of Romans 8:28. Horatius Bonar, the nineteenth-century Scottish pastor and hymn writer, knew a lot about this spirit when he wrote:

He who is carrying it on is not one who can be baffled and forced to give up His design. He is able to carry it out in the unlikeliest circumstances and against the most resolute resistance. Everything must give way before Him. This thought is, I confess, to me one of the most comforting connected with the discipline. If it could fail! If God could be frustrated in His designs after we have suffered so much, it would be awful! ... [but] God's treatment *must* succeed. It cannot miscarry or be frustrated even in its most arduous efforts, even in reference to its minutest objects. It is the mighty power of God that is at work within and upon us, and this is our consolation. ... All is love, all is wisdom, and all is faithfulness, yet all is also power (*When God's Children Suffer* [New Canaan, Conn.: Keats Publishing, 1981], 30–31. Cited in Jerry Bridges, *Trusting God* [Colorado Springs: NavPress, 1988], 176).

During a particular time of testing or suffering, God may seem distant or disinterested in our plight. That's because our human emotions can override trust in God's truth, and we can come to believe that no outcome to our present situation is desirable for us. Job, on the other hand, shows us the kind of endurance and patience that is eager to trust God and learn whatever lessons His sovereign purpose desires us to learn. It was that very trust that caused him to glorify God at the conclusion to his time of suffering:

I know that Thou canst do all things, and that no purpose of Thine can be thwarted. "Who is this that hides counsel without knowledge?" Therefore I have declared that which I did not understand, things too wonderful for me, which I did not know. "Hear, now, and I will speak; I will ask Thee, and do Thou instruct me." I have heard of Thee by the hearing of the ear; but now my eye sees Thee; therefore I retract, and I repent in dust and ashes (Job 42:2-6).

As a result of patience and unwavering trust during his long ordeal, Job gained a new understanding of his sovereign God and a greater reassurance of the joys of being dealt with as one of His children. It is this joy that I want to focus on first in our look at the lessons from suffering.

## SUFFERING PRODUCES FRESH JOY

We have already seen how it is possible, by grace, to rejoice in the midst of suffering. It is also true that the joy we experience from our trials can be some of the greatest joy we ever know. Since one of the major reasons God sends trials into the believer's life is to test the very genuineness of his faith (Gen. 22), what more fitting occasion to have joy than in the aftermath of an experience of suffering that has proved the reality of our salvation? A strengthened assurance of our salvation and confidence that God cares for us, as manifest in the reality that our suffering could neither break our faith nor sever us from His love, is cause for the highest happiness.

In his first letter written to believers who were suffering persecution, the Apostle Peter clearly affirms the close connection between suffering and the assurance of salvation:

Blessed be the God and Father of our Lord Jesus Christ, who according to His great mercy has caused us to be born again to a living hope through the resurrection of Jesus Christ from the dead, to obtain an inheritance which is imperishable and undefiled and will not fade away, reserved in heaven for you, who are protected by the power of God through faith for a salvation ready to be revealed in the last time. In this you greatly rejoice, even though now for a little while, if necessary, you have been distressed by various trials, that the proof of your faith, being more precious than gold which is perishable, even though tested by fire, may be found to result in praise and glory and honor at the revelation of Jesus Christ (1 Peter 1:3-7).

True joy does not come cheaply or as a fleeting, superficial emotion. Real joy is produced by much deeper factors than the circumstances that produce superficial happiness. Christians who struggle through the negative circumstances of life, floundering in doubt and dismay, have forgotten that genuine joy awaits them from the confidence that their lives are hid with Christ in God. In God's providence, that joy and assurance can be most strong in a time of suffering.

Peter gives several perspectives that will help us gain a fresh appreciation for the joy of our salvation.

### Confidence in Our Protected Inheritance

One reality that Peter offers as incentive for having joy—no matter what we may have endured—is *confidence in our protected inheritance*. He describes this inheritance in 1 Peter 1:4 as one that is "imperishable and undefiled and will not fade away, reserved in heaven." And this great confidence is something we can "greatly rejoice" in (v. 6). This key term is very expressive in the original and much stronger than the usual word translated "rejoice." It means to be super abundantly happy in the richest sense. (The *King James* translates it "be exceedingly glad" in Matt. 5:12.) The term is always used in the New Testament in reference to a spiritual joy that comes from a relationship with God, never of a temporal joy (or circumstantial happiness) that results from other relationships.

Peter assures us that suffering is indeed positive because it is so integrally tied to assurance of salvation. Jesus' disciples had difficulty with this truth, as was evident when He was teaching them in the Upper Room. In response to their confusion and apprehension concerning His imminent death, burial, and resurrection, Jesus told them: "Truly, truly, I say to you, that you will weep and lament, but the world will rejoice; you will be sorrowful, but your sorrow will be turned to joy. Whenever a woman is in travail she has sorrow, because her hour has come; but when she gives birth to the child, she remembers the anguish no more, for joy that a child has been born into the world. Therefore you, too, now have sorrow; but I will see you again, and your heart will rejoice, and no one takes your joy away from you" (John 16:20-22). He told the disciples there was reason to rejoice because of what He promised them in the future when the suffering would be over. Their time of grief when Jesus died turned into tremendous joy when they saw Him again and came to grips with the significance of His resurrection.

We are encouraged by Paul's words in Ephesians 1:11-13, "We have obtained an inheritance . . . to the end that we who were the first to hope in Christ should be to the praise of His glory.... having also believed, you were sealed in Him with the Holy Spirit of promise." The Spirit of God dwelling in us is the guarantee of our protected inheritance.

Whenever we have endured a period of suffering or trial, it tends to make us long for our eternal inheritance. Our joy will not always be automatic and we cannot deny that real pain and sorrow accompanies suffering, but in the long run it's a matter of which way we look. The believer's response to trials can be compared to riding on a train. Imagine that you're in the observation car of a train passing through the mountains. On the left side the train is passing very close to a high mountain and all you can see is a dark shadow. On the right side the train is passing a magnificent view of valleys, meadows, streams, and lakes, stretching as far as the eye can see. Some people on this train, just as some in life, will look only to the left, at the dark mountain. But some will choose to look to the right and take advantage of the splendid and uplifting scenery.

Too often believers choose to focus on the negatives of their circumstances and the dark moments of their times of trial and suffering. First they concentrate on the negatives *while* the train is in the tunnel of difficulty. But compounding their sorrow they continue to look to the mountain shadows of their trial *after* the train has left the tunnel behind. In so doing, such Christians forfeit the joy that is theirs had they only looked to the brightness and certainty of their eternal inheritance in Christ. Again, it is simply a choice to look ahead. Nothing in this life can take away an eternal inheritance in heaven's glory. As Peter says, it is "reserved" in heaven for us. The reservation was made by

God, purchased by Jesus Christ, and is now guaranteed by the Holy Spirit (as suggested in the opening to this chapter).

### Confidence in a Proven Faith

Perhaps the greatest positive result that can come from suffering is a fresh sense of joyful confidence that our faith is genuine. That is Peter's second perspective: *trials and sufferings prove our faith*. When we successfully persevere through the period of suffering, God affirms to us the strength of our saving faith.

In 1 Peter 1:7, Peter uses an earthly illustration to demonstrate how valuable a proven faith is as a source of rejoicing. He says it is "more precious than gold which is perishable, even though tested by fire." In biblical times gold was fashioned into a variety of practical as well as decorative items. It was the most highly valued metal, and it was also the standard for all monetary transactions. (Even in modern times, until the 1930s, the United States and other industrialized nations used a gold standard. In this system the nation's currency has a value measured in gold, and it can be exchanged for gold.) So Peter chose an item his readers would instantly recognize as the most valuable metal and said that even when processed by fire to the highest level of purity, it was still not as precious as a proven faith. Gold, even the most highly refined, simply cannot pass the test of eternity. But our faith can.

## SUFFERING ENHANCES FUTURE GLORY

God brings sufferings, trials, persecutions, and other kinds of adversity as vital events in our spiritual growth process. The following familiar verses in James

1:2-4 confirm this truth succinctly: "Consider it all joy, my brethren, when you encounter various trials, knowing that the testing of your faith produces endurance. And let endurance have its perfect result, that you may be perfect and complete, lacking in nothing." That refers primarily to our Christian pilgrimage on earth. But Peter bridges present suffering to future glory when he says that God, who has called us to glory, will "perfect, confirm, strengthen and establish you" (1 Peter 5:10).

As long as we are in this world, we are called to bear suffering patiently and see it through to God's ultimate purpose. That's when we begin to see that suffering is beneficial—it is part of our final perfection and glorification. We took some glimpses earlier in the book and earlier in this chapter at the relationship between present suffering and future glory. Now let's take a closer look at this relationship, for it profoundly affects how we view the result of any particular incident of suffering in our lives.

Suffering teaches patience, but that's not all. In light of eternity, patience is not the primary thing we need to grasp, because in heaven we will have no need to exercise patience. God is far more pleased if we learn this principle: what we suffer now is directly related to our capacity to glorify Him in eternity. After all, praising, honoring, adoring, and glorifying God will be our eternal function (Rev. 4–5), so we should be concerned with whatever impact events in our life have on that future reality.

The Apostle Paul enhances our understanding: "If we endure, we shall also reign with Him" (2 Tim. 2:12). The point is simply that the greater endurance we develop through suffering in this life, the greater the eternal reward we will realize in the next life. I firmly believe that this eternal reward is primarily our capacity to glorify God throughout eternity. Therefore, the greater the endurance now, the greater the capacity to glorify Him later.

Jesus applied this principle when teaching James and John about their positions in the kingdom of God (Matt. 20:20-23). The two disciples approached Jesus through their mother and wanted Him to appoint one of them to sit on His right and the other to sit on His left in the kingdom. In other words, they were asking for the positions of greatest prominence and reward— the highest ones any of His brethren could hold in Christ's kingdom. They obviously recognized the concept of rankings or rewards in the kingdom and Jesus did not disagree with that interpretation, because it was right (1 Cor. 3:9-15; 2 Cor. 5:10; 2 John 8). However, He did need to correct their understanding regarding how, within God's plan, the concept worked: "Jesus answered and said, 'You do not know what you are asking for. Are you able to drink the cup that I am about to drink?' They said to Him, 'We are able.' He said to them, 'My cup you shall drink; but to sit on My right and on My left, this is not Mine to give, but it is for those for whom it has been prepared by My Father' " (Matt. 20:22-23).

The cup Jesus refers to is His suffering and death. He is asking rhetorically if the brothers would be able to drink that cup if they wanted to sit on His right and left. The implication is that suffering and elevation in the kingdom are directly correlated. (Christ suffered the most in His crucifixion and He was elevated to the highest position, the right hand of the Father.) If the disciples had their eyes set on great prominence and high rewards in eternity, they had to know the path to that end is marked by great suffering and endurance.

The lesson for us is that whenever we suffer and emerge patiently and faithfully from it, God is pleased because we are increasing our eternal capacity to glorify Him. We too should take great pleasure and joy in the outcome of a time of suffering, trial, or persecution, realizing that we are enhancing our heavenly reward and understanding more about the power of suffering (see Rev. 2:10).

## SUFFERING PRODUCES TRUE COMFORT

Several summers ago I had the joy of visiting Ireland, the "Emerald Isle." It is nicknamed that for good reason because it has perhaps the greenest countryside of any place in the world. The green land results from the amount of mist and fog that sometimes obscures its usually soft and gentle landscape. This phenomenon is a parallel to the Christian life. Oftentimes when a believer's life is shrouded by suffering and sorrow, there is a fresh beauty of soul underneath. As we have seen with the Apostle Paul's example, gentle and tender hearts are the product of great troubles. God allows troubles and sufferings so that He might give us much comfort and we can comfort others.

The Lord is the only one who can give us that supreme comfort. Second Corinthians 1:3-4 says, "Blessed be the God and Father of our Lord Jesus Christ, the Father of mercies and God of all comfort; who comforts us in all our affliction so that we may be able to comfort those who are in any affliction with the comfort with which we ourselves are comforted by God."

Paul, based on his own experiences, has some simple yet profound things to say (2 Cor. 1:3-8) about comfort as it relates to suffering. First, he reaffirms the basic promise that God will comfort us (vv. 3-4; see also Ps. 23:4; Isa. 40:1; 49:13; 51:3; 61:2; Matt. 5:4; Acts 9:31). In Romans 8:32 he says: "He who did not spare His own Son, but delivered Him up for us all, how will He not also with Him freely give us all things?" The clear application is that if God the Father has already given us His greatest gift, His Son Jesus Christ, then it is no problem for Him to give us comparatively small servings of His comfort.

God's comfort comes to us not as an end in itself nor merely for our own benefit. Second Corinthians 1:4 indicates a definite purpose: "so that we may be able to comfort those who are in any affliction." Comfort, therefore, is something that God entrusts to us so that we can share it with others. And it is entrusted to us in direct proportion to the amount and intensity of suffering we endure, which means the more we suffer, the more we're comforted; and the more we're comforted, the more we can be comforters. The Apostle Paul was certainly a testimony to this principle—he suffered as much as any man (2 Cor. 11:23-27) and yet ministered to others in the gentleness of Jesus Christ (Phil. 1:8) and with the tenderness of a nursing mother (1 Thes. 2:7).

God's comfort, as great as it is, does have some boundaries. Just as Peter correlated godly benefits and rewards with the right kind of suffering, other Scripture clearly implies that we can and should expect divine comfort only if we are suffering for righteousness (2 Cor. 1:5). It logically follows that we can't be true comforters if we ourselves have not experienced suffering and comfort within God's limits—as Christians for Christ's sake. Paul is again our example (4:11-15).

Finally, one of the most cherished by-products that genuine comfort will give us is the assurance of a partnership in suffering. As part of the body of Christ we are not alone and do not experience suffering in a vacuum. Partnership in suffering is vital. If comfort allows us to be comforters, then obviously other people are being affected by the outcome of our suffering experience. The partnership concept fills out the role we can have as a comforter. That is Paul's point when he says,

> But if we are afflicted, it is for your comfort and salvation; or if we are comforted, it is for your comfort, which is effective in the patient enduring of the same sufferings which we also suffer; and our hope for you is firmly grounded, knowing that as you are sharers of our sufferings, so also you are sharers of our comfort (1:6-7).

That is a portrait of mutuality, connectedness, and solidarity among a group of believers (Paul and the Corinthians) who knew and would know the reality of suffering. It is also motivation for us to be encouraged as we emerge from any period of suffering. The comfort we receive from the Lord helps us look beyond ourselves and reminds us that others in our local body can benefit from our comfort. These other believers can in turn be a comfort to us later on as they go through their own trials. Therefore, all our sufferings enable us to minister to each other in genuine body life fashion. (This principle of partnership in suffering is an extended application of 1 Cor. 12, especially v. 26.)

## SUFFERING YIELDS GREATER WISDOM

Wisdom has always been one of the most valued character traits that a believer could possess. The case of

Solomon is especially appropriate. First there is the well-known account of his asking God for wisdom (1 Kings 3:5-13). Then there is the fact of his authorship of Wisdom literature in the Bible (Ecc. and portions of Prov.). Another important Old Testament figure who appreciated the value of wisdom was Job, who learned it amidst severe suffering.

He learned to recognize the bankruptcy of his reason and even the inadequacy of other's advice and came to understand that God's wisdom was the source for understanding all of life and its problems. Here is what Job said about the unsurpassed value of divine wisdom:

> But where can wisdom be found? And where is the place of understanding? Man does not know its value, nor is it found in the land of the living. The deep says, "It is not in me"; and the sea says, "It is not with me." Pure gold cannot be given in exchange for it, nor can silver be weighed as its price. It cannot be valued in the gold of Ophir, in precious onyx, or sapphire. Gold or glass cannot equal it, nor can it be exchanged for articles of fine gold. Coral and crystal are not to be mentioned; and the acquisition of wisdom is above that of pearls. The topaz of Ethiopia cannot equal it, nor can it be valued in pure gold. Where then does wisdom come from? And where is the place of understanding? . . . God understands its way; and He knows its place. For He looks to the ends of the earth, and sees everything under the heavens. . . . And to man He said, "Behold, the fear of the Lord, that is wisdom; and to depart from evil is understanding" (Job 28:12-20, 23-24, 28).

Wisdom from God pulls everything together during suffering, helps us to endure it, and allows us to have a right perspective. But wisdom is something we must not presume will be ours or that we can gain in our own strength. James informed of the means to obtain wisdom when he wrote: "But if any of you lacks wisdom, let him ask of God, who gives to all men generously and without reproach, and it will be given to him" (1:5).

Of course, the kind of wisdom James is referring to is not a detached academic knowledge or some philosophical speculation. Instead, it corresponds to what the Wisdom literature teaches: Wisdom is the practical understanding of how to live life in obedience to the will and Word of God and for His glory (Prov. 3:5-7; 4:11; 8:12; 10:8; 14:8).

In the context of suffering, therefore, we need to ask God for wisdom to help us persevere scripturally. We need His help to see sovereignty and providence working in our situation, to have a joyful attitude, and to respond submissively. This need for help dovetails marvelously with one of the overall purposes God has in allowing sufferings and trials: to make us more dependent on Him. Such dependency is synonymous with prayer, which is implied in the phrase "let him ask of God" (James 1:5). The Lord is very generous with the wisdom we require—James says He "gives to all men generously [unconditionally]"—and all His resources, and He desires to pour out on us everything that is beneficial (Prov. 2:2-7; Jer. 29:11-13; Matt. 7:7-11).

## SUFFERING YIELDS TRUE HUMILITY

One of the most humbling, yet least regarded, truths concerning sufferings is that they do not exclude favorites. This principle operates all through the natural world. Disasters, accidents, crimes, diseases, economic recessions, and wars affect people of all classes. In the recent earthquakes that struck Kobe, Japan and Southern California, thousands of homes and businesses in all sections of the quake areas were damaged or destroyed. Rich and poor alike were similarly affected by transportation disruptions in the first weeks following the quakes. Expensive homes and modest apartments were each subjected to significant damage.

The realization that difficulty does not discriminate tends to sober and humble believers as well. Again James speaks to poor and rich believers being affected by the humbling nature of trials and sufferings, dealing first with the attitude of the believer of modest means: "But let the brother of humble circumstances glory in his high position" (James 1:9). For poor Christians, poverty itself can be an ongoing trial. For them the challenge is not in realizing the humility of suffering, but in remembering that they can rejoice in their exalted spiritual position as Christians (1 Peter 1:3-6). Economic deprivation does not detract from the glorious inheritance to be received in the next life (Eph. 1:11-14).

The wealthier Christian, on the other hand, does have the challenge of accepting the humiliation that results from trials and sufferings: "And let the rich man glory in his humiliation, because like flowering grass he will pass away" (James 1:10). Those of us who are better off materially need to welcome trials because they remind us that our true dependency is on God and His grace, not in our privileged economic status. The humiliation of trials will also remind us that earthly riches are temporary; they fade away like grass.

Therefore, there is a great leveling factor at work in

the process of sufferings, trials, and persecutions. True humility teaches all believers, whether of high position or low, to say with sincerity, "My resources are in God." R.C.H. Lenski, the conservative Lutheran commentator, summarizes this equalizing principle well:

> Faith in Christ lifts the lowly brother beyond his trials to the great height of a position in the Kingdom of Christ, where as God's child he is rich and may rejoice and boast. Faith in Christ does an equally blessed thing for the rich brother: it fills him with the Spirit of Christ, the spirit of lowliness and true Christian humility.... As the poor brother forgets all his earthly poverty, so the rich brother forgets all his earthly riches. The two are equals by faith in Christ (*The Interpretation of the Epistle to the Hebrews and the Epistle of James* [Minneapolis: Augsburg, 1966], 534–35).

It is always a challenge for believers to keep their hearts and minds focused properly through a difficult trial or time of suffering. Even with the promise of lessons learned and rewards realized, the certainty of these benefits can seem more theoretical than real. But we can have a much greater confidence in the reality of all these things if we simply remember these words: "For we live by faith, not by sight" (2 Cor. 5:7). God's purposes are not always apparent at the start of a trial, but that need not deter us from keeping our eyes on Him. Those mentioned in faith's "hall of fame" in Hebrews 11 were enabled to see beyond the immediate obstacles to the ultimate prize (see especially vv. 13-16).

Christians in modern times have also comprehended how essential it is to trust in God's sovereignty through all circumstances. William Cowper was an eighteenth-century English poet and hymn writer with a naturally melancholy disposition. In spite of his sufferings and struggles, Cowper ministered as a lay assistant to the great John Newton and wrote sixty-eight hymns. One of those, "God Moves in a Mysterious Way," expresses well the mind-set all believers should have toward life and its difficulties.

> God moves in a mysterious way His wonders to
> perform;
> He plants His footsteps in the sea, and rides upon
> the storm.
> Deep in unfathomable mines of never-failing skill
> He treasures up His bright designs, and works
> His sovereign will.
>
> Ye fearful saints, fresh courage take;
> the clouds ye so much dread
> are big with mercy and shall break
> in blessings on your head.
>
> Judge not the Lord by feeble sense,
> but trust Him for His grace;
> behind a frowning providence
> He hides a smiling face.
>
> His purposes will ripen fast,
> unfolding ev'ry hour;
> the bud may have a bitter taste,
> but sweet will be the flow'r.
>
> Blind unbelief is sure to err,
> and scan His work in vain;
> God is His own interpreter,
> and He will make it plain.

# Personal and Group Study Guide

**For Personal Study**

Settle into your favorite chair with your Bible, a pen or pencil, and this book. Read a chapter, marking portions that seem significant to you. Write in the margins. Note where you agree, disagree, or question the author. Look up footnotes and relevant Scripture passages. Then turn to the questions listed in this study guide. If you want to trace your progress with a written record, use a notebook to record your answers, thoughts, feelings, and further questions. Refer to the text and to the Scriptures as you allow the questions to enlarge your thinking. And pray. Ask God to give you a discerning mind for truth, an active concern for others, and a greater love for Himself.

**For Group Study**

**Plan ahead.** Before meeting with your group, read and mark the chapter as if you were preparing for personal study. Glance through the questions making mental notes of how you might contribute to your group's discussion. Bring a Bible and the text to your meeting.

**Arrange an environment that promotes discussion.** Comfortable chairs arranged in a casual circle invite people to talk with each other. Then say, "We are here to listen and respond to each other—and to learn together." If you are the leader, simply be sure to sit where you can have eye contact with each person.

**Promptness counts.** Time is as valuable to many people as money. If the group runs late (because of a late start), these people will feel as robbed as if you had picked their pockets. So, unless you have mutual agreement, begin and end on time.

**Involve everyone.** Group learning works best if everyone participates more or less equally. If you are a natural *talker*, pause before you enter the conversation. Then ask a quiet person what he or she thinks. If you are a natural *listener*, don't hesitate to jump into the discussion. Others will benefit from your thoughts—but only if you speak them. If you are the *leader*, be careful not to dominate the session. Of course, you will have thought about the study ahead of time, but don't assume that people are present just to hear you—as flattering as that may feel. Instead, help group members to make their own discoveries. Ask the questions, but insert your own ideas only as they are needed to fill gaps.

**Pace the study.** The questions for each session are designed to last about one hour. Early questions form the framework for later discussion, so don't rush by so quickly that you miss a valuable foundation. Later questions, however, often speak of the here and now. So don't dawdle so long at the beginning that you leave no time to "get personal." While the leader must take responsibility for timing the flow of questions, it is the job of each person in the group to assist in keeping the study moving at an even pace.

**Pray for each other—together, or alone.** Then watch

God's hand at work in all of your lives.

Notice that each session includes the following features:

**Session Topic**—a brief statement summarizing the session.

**Community Builder**—an activity to get acquainted with the session topic and/or with each other.

**Questions**—a list of questions to encourage individual or group discovery and application.

**Prayer Focus**—suggestions for turning one's learning into prayer.

**Optional Activities**—supplemental ideas that will enhance the study.

**Assignment**—activities or preparation to complete prior to the next session.

# ONE

# *Suffering in the Plan of God*

**Session Topic**
In God's sovereign plan Christians will encounter some amount of suffering.

**Community Builder** (*Choose One*)
1. What was the most recent piece of bad news that really bothered you? Why did it make you so upset?
2. What is the most challenging aspect that you can recall from your own past experience of adversity? Why was it so difficult?

**Group Discovery Questions**
1. What did Jesus predict in Matthew 5:10-12?
2. As used in John 15 and other places in the New Testament, what does the term *world* refer to?
3. What truth about today's culture is reflected in what Paul observed in Acts 17?
4. What biblical concept is the key to having a clearer perspective on suffering?
5. What does Genesis 22 illustrate in regard to the reasons for trials and suffering?
6. How should we assess Paul's reaction to his unidentified infirmity in 2 Corinthians 12:7-10?
7. What does Jesus warn against in Matthew 6:24? How is this especially applicable to contemporary society?
8. What does Hebrews 11:24-26 say about Moses' example?
9. What incentive should Romans 8:18-25 give us in regard to our dealing with suffering?

10. What significance does Luke 14:26-27 have concerning the purpose of suffering?

11. Reread Hebrews 5:7-10 and Philippians 2:8-9. What do these passages say about what Jesus learned from suffering?

### Focus on Prayer

- Ask God to help you resolve any doubts you may have concerning the reality of His sovereignty over all things.
- Thank the Lord for His plans for your future well-being (Rom. 8:18-25).
- Pray that the other members of your group will be strengthened when they face suffering.

### Optional Activities

1. Read James 4:13-16 and discuss what it says about presumption and our personal plans. Which of your plans would be most affected by unexpected adversity? Look at your schedule for the next week and commit each item on it into His care.

2. It is easy to be frightened at the prospect of persecution. But 1 John 4:4 tells us that we have adequate resources to face the sinful world system. Have you ever experienced persecution for your faith? If so, how did you react? How could you have been better prepared?

### Assignment

1. Memorize 1 Peter 4:19.
2. Read chapter 2 of *The Power of Suffering*.

# TWO

# *Examples of Faith in the Fire*

## Session Topic
Through superior role models we can learn much about how to deal well with suffering.

## Community Builder *(Choose One)*
1. Who was the first role model you can remember? Did that person become a favorite example for you?
2. See if you can list at least five prominent people from the popular culture (music, entertainment, sports) whom you would consider as role models.

## Group Discovery Questions
1. What were two key features of Stephen's ministry prior to his death?
2. Acts 6:15 says Stephen's face was "like the face of an angel." In what other ways could we describe and compare his facial expression?
3. What does it mean to be filled with the Spirit? (Eph. 5:18) (pp. 49–50)
4. How did Daniel and his three friends adapt to their circumstances in Babylon?
5. How did Shadrach, Meshach, and Abed-nego display their inner convictions before the intense pressure of Nebuchadnezzar? (see Job 13:15; Ps. 119:11)
6. What does Daniel 6:4-9 reveal about the actions of Daniel's enemies?
7. What does Daniel 6:16 suggest about Daniel's relationship to King Darius?
8. If you knew that you were about to enter a period of suffering, how would you begin to prepare?

**Prayer Focus**
- Set aside some time to pray for believers in other parts of the world who face opposition because of their stand for Christ.
- Reflect again on Stephen's life. Thank God for the testimony Stephen's life and ministry had on the church.
- Pray that God will give you the discipline to be more like Daniel and his friends in your Christian walk.

**Optional Activities**
1. Read 1 Timothy 3 and list the qualifications it mentions for church leadership. What qualities are you strong in? In which ones do you need to improve?
2. Think of the many excuses our society offers for not putting God first. Which ones do you think have the strongest influence? During the next month keep track in writing of the times when you felt tempted not to put God first in a particular situation. Read Luke 14:16-24 and meditate on its application for you.

**Assignment**
1. Compare and contrast aspects in the life of Joseph (Gen. 37–50) with the character traits of the men discussed here in chapter 2. Write down your findings.
2. Read chapter 3 in *The Power of Suffering*.

# THREE

# Paul: A Profile in Suffering

## Session Topic
Because of his own experiences, the Apostle Paul is a superb example of godly perseverance through all kinds of adversity.

## Community Builder (*Choose One*)
1. Do you have stick-to-itiveness? That's an old-fashioned slang term for perseverance. Do you tend to be easily discouraged when the going gets tough? Or are you more likely to look at the bright side and keep going? When do you most feel like quitting?
2. Do you find it easy or difficult to talk about death with a family member? Explain your answer.

## Group Discovery Questions
1. What common trait is found in Galatians 5:22; Philippians 4:4; and 1 Thessalonians 5:16?
2. What was Paul's status as he wrote to the Philippians? (Phil. 1:7; cf. Acts 28:30-31)
3. How is Acts 16:22-33 illustrative and representative of the theme of chapter 3?
4. What are detractors? How did they affect Paul's ministry? (p. 72)
5. What distinct possibility does Paul allude to in Philippians 1:19-21?
6. How much confidence did Paul have in God's Word? Why? (p. 75)
7. What does Philippians 1:19 mean when it uses the word "provision"? How is it applicable to Paul and us?

8. What promises of Jesus did Paul trust in? (p. 77)

9. What was Paul's strategy in figuratively comparing himself to a clay pot?

10. In 2 Corinthians 4:8-9, what four paradoxes in the midst of suffering does Paul list? (p. 79–81)

11. In what three ways was Paul able to realize endurance in suffering? (p. 83)

## Prayer Focus

- Are you dealing with a particular trial that is wearing down your endurance? Or perhaps you know of someone else who is in the midst of a trial or suffering. Spend some time in prayer each day this week asking God to strengthen you or the other person during this difficulty (Gal. 6:9).

- Pray for the pastor of your church that he will have spiritual stamina in carrying out his ministry.

- Pray that you will have an attitude of joy next week, no matter what challenges you will face.

## Optional Activities

1. Read a book about contemporary Christian role models who endured martyrdom (Jim Elliot, *Through Gates of Splendor*) or suffering and hardship (Joni Eareckson Tada, *A Step Further*).

2. Memorize 2 Timothy 3:16-17 as a reminder of the confidence you can have in Scripture during any situation.

## Assignment

1. Read John 15–16. Make a list of all the promises that Jesus makes to His followers in these chapters. Make a separate list of the ones that apply most directly to trials and suffering.

2. Read chapter 4 of *The Power of Suffering*.

# FOUR

# The Silence of the Lamb of God

## Session Topic
Jesus Christ is the only role model Christians really need for how to deal with suffering.

## Community Builder (*Choose One*)
1. Think of a situation when you spoke out (perhaps defensively) when you should have kept quiet. How did you feel afterwards? Is it always best to remain silent when criticized?
2. Of the various images that non-Christians have of Jesus, which one seems most common to you? How do you respond when you hear it mentioned?

## Group Discovery Questions
1. What comfort is there for us as we face hostility from the world? Look at John 15:18-21 and Matthew 10:21-25 again. What are a couple of differences in detail that you see between the two passages?
2. What major misconception did Jesus' disciples reveal concerning the cause of suffering (John 9)? In spite of this, do you think they would have been better counselors to Job than his friends were? Why or why not?
3. The word "example" in 1 Peter 2:21 suggests the idea of following a model. How closely do you need to copy a model or diagram when you're building something? What happens if you disregard the model?
4. Do you agree with the statement, "The first and most readily apparent place that sin shows itself is the human mouth"? (p. 96) Explain your answer.

5. What major character trait does Isaiah 53 reveal about the Suffering Servant? What other truths can be drawn from that chapter?

6. What one sentence do you especially appreciate in this chapter? Why?

7. What does Acts 23:3-5 show us about Paul? Would your reaction be the same in a similar situation?

8. Think of the many things in everyday life that we entrust our well-being and safety to. Most of us are also very trusting of other people in business contexts. How can 1 Peter 2:23 motivate us to entrust ourselves more fully to God?

9. With the example of Hugh Latimer as an inspiration, can you think of a time when you were able to encourage a fellow believer in the midst of a trying situation? What was the outcome?

### Prayer Focus

- Give thanks for Christ's willingness to suffer and die on your behalf.
- Ask God to give you a more Christlike attitude during those times when you encounter unjust criticism or opposition.
- Pray, asking the Lord through His Spirit to reveal to you areas of pride that would hinder your testimony in the midst of a personal trial.

### Optional Activities

1. Read one of the Gospel accounts of Jesus' suffering and death. Note on paper the various ways He was the ideal example of how to react to suffering.

2. Study Job 1:1–2:11. Write a brief summary in your own words to show that this passage denies the notion that all suffering is caused by sin.

**Assignment**
1. Memorize Isaiah 53:7.
2. Read chapter 5 of *The Power of Suffering*.

# FIVE

# *Preparing for Suffering*

## Session Topic
Christian discipleship is the crucial element in being prepared to face sufferings and trials.

## Community Builder *(Choose One)*
1. How do you prepare for or look ahead to a typical week at work or school? What's one practical step you regularly take to ensure your success?
2. On a scale from one to ten (one being almost nonexistent, ten being as good as humanly possible) rate your own spiritual preparedness. How does this correlate with your current level of discipleship?

## Group Discovery Questions
1. Have you ever experienced a major natural disaster? What was it like? What would you do differently next time to be more prepared?
2. Think of someone, past or present, whom you have really liked as a teacher, coach, boss, etc. How could you apply the principles of Matthew 10:24 to that relationship?
3. Are you pursuing the goal of becoming more like Christ? Read and reflect on Philippians 3:14-17.
4. What common thread of truth runs through Proverbs 29:25; John 14:27; and 2 Timothy 1:7-8?
5. What comfort does Isaiah 26:3-4 provide?
6. What does Jesus warn of in Matthew 10:34-37? Will it happen to everyone?
7. What positive result comes from grateful prayer? (Phil. 4:6-7)

8. How would you define God's providence? (pp. 114–15) State the main difference between it and a miracle.

9. What two basic elements are necessary for the Christian to be prepared for Satan's attacks? (1 Peter 5:8-9)

## Prayer Focus

- Spend some time in prayer asking God's Spirit to show you any areas in which your spiritual preparedness is weak. Ask Him for the strength to make improvements.
- Pray for your group that each member will be more fearless in his walk with God in the coming month.
- If you are dealing with spiritual opposition from some member of your family, ask God for wisdom and strength in coping with it. If you are not in that situation, pray for another person who is facing such opposition.

## Optional Activities

1. Read *The Pursuit of Holiness* by Jerry Bridges. (If you have already read that one, read Bridges' sequel, *The Practice of Godliness.*)

2. Watch your local Christian television channel several times next week. Listen for and make notes on how many times someone mentions the reality of spiritual warfare. Was the discussion or comment scriptural and balanced each time?

## Assignment

1. Read Ephesians 6:10-18. Meditate each day next week on a different part of God's armory. Write down your key insights and ways God wants you to apply them.

2. Read chapter 6 of *The Power of Suffering.*

## SIX

# *Dealing with Suffering*

**Session Topic**
We need to have the right attitude as we deal with suffering.

**Community Builder** *(Choose One)*
1. Name one aspect of your home or work situation that gives you the most struggle to maintain a good attitude. When and how did it last present a challenge?
2. How well do you handle surprises? What response first comes to mind when you're faced with an unexpected change of schedule?

**Group Discovery Questions**
1. In general, how well do you think the average believer does in applying what he learns from Scripture?
2. What does the "fiery ordeal" in 1 Peter 4:12 symbolize?
3. How could having joy in the midst of suffering or persecution lead to a pharisaical attitude? What kind of perspective on suffering would help prevent that? (p. 123)
4. Explain what Peter meant when he wrote about sharing in the sufferings of Christ. (p. 124)
5. How can dealing well with suffering be an incentive for us to welcome the return of Christ? (1 Peter 4:13)
6. Give at least three Old Testament illustrations of when God's Spirit was shown to His people (p. 125). How does the Spirit demonstrate His presence for us today?

7. Reread the excerpt about Thomas Cranmer's death (p. 126). What impresses you most about how he handled death?

8. What does the term "troublesome meddler" in 1 Peter 4:15 primarily refer to? What else might it mean?

9. According to 1 Peter 4:7, 17, how are we to understand the times in which we live?

10. Consider the original meaning of the word "entrust" in 1 Peter 4:19 (p. 131). What confidence does it give us in the trustworthiness of God, especially in suffering?

### Prayer Focus

- Pray that God will give you a proper, biblical attitude in everything.
- Take some time to praise and thank God for all His resources that help you deal with unexpected adversity.
- Pray that God will make you more discerning in the face of various trials and sufferings, not only in your own life but also in counseling others.

### Optional Activities

1. Make a brief study of the pro-life movement. Look at some back issues of Christian magazines (*Christianity Today, Moody Magazine, World*) that would have news reports or articles about various strategies used by different wings of the movement. Which strategy seems most biblical? Use Scripture to support your answers.

2. Send a note of encouragement to an individual or family you know who is enduring a difficult trial right now. If you don't know of anyone who is currently in a difficulty, share with a Christian friend one thing you learned in this chapter.

**Assignment**

1. Read Matthew 5:1-17. Reflect and meditate on all the ways this passage can be an encouragement in facing hostility from the world. Memorize two or three of the most meaningful verses.

2. Read chapter 7 of *The Power of Suffering*.

# *The Lessons from Suffering*

## Session Topic

We should not only be aware of the reality of suffering, but also be eager to embrace the lessons that come from it.

## Community Builder *(Choose One)*

1. Recall a frustrating experience when you had to relearn, perhaps the hard way, a lesson you should have grasped from an earlier trial. What do you remember most vividly about the second experience?

2. Do you think it's more difficult for a wealthy Christian to face suffering? What extra obstacles might he face?

## Group Discovery Questions

1. What truth from chapter 1 does Horatius Bonar's quote reemphasize? (p. 136)

2. How has the strength of your assurance of salvation grown?

3. How would you define the term "greatly rejoice" in 1 Peter 1:6? (p. 139) Use your own words to clarify the idea.

4. Who and what guarantees our spiritual inheritance? (Eph. 1:11-14)

5. What example is used in 1 Peter 1:7 to illustrate how valuable a proven faith is?

6. Why is patience not the most important lesson to learn from suffering? What is a more far-reaching principle we need to understand?

7. How much did James and John understand about

the future kingdom of God? (Matt. 20–23) What truth did Jesus need to clarify for them?

8. Can you recall an instance in which God's comfort was especially meaningful to you? Were you afterward able to comfort someone else in a similar fashion?

9. What value does the world place on wisdom? Compare the usefulness of wisdom versus knowledge.

10. Can you identify with William Cowper? (p. 151) Why or why not?

### Prayer Focus

- Thank God that He has a purpose and plan for any suffering you will have to deal with.
- Ask the Lord for an opportunity within the next month to minister comfort to someone who is in, or has recently endured, a time of suffering.
- Pray that you and everyone else in your group would seek to have wisdom and humility as you all endure various trials.

### Optional Activities

1. William Cowper's hymn "God Moves in a Mysterious Way" is not in many modern hymnals. Write out each verse on an index card and memorize one verse each week for the next five weeks.

2. Read and study Proverbs 1–3. Based on these chapters, compose a brief definition of wisdom, record your findings concerning the advantages of wisdom, and write down some of the main characteristics of the wise person.

### Assignment

1. Memorize Romans 8:35-39 or James 1:2-6.

2. Complete one of the Optional Activities, which you may not have had time to do, from earlier in the study.

# SCRIPTURE INDEX

**Genesis**
1:27    *129*
18:1-3    *57*
18:25    *23, 99*
22:1-2    *26*
22:3-8    *27*
22:9-12    *28*
50:19-21    *116*
50:20    *47*

**Exodus**
17:16    *24*
20:2-6    *55*
21:22-25    *129*
33:7-11    *48*
33:17-23    *48*
34:29-35    *48*

**Deuteronomy**
4:15-19    *55*
6:5    *37*
13:3    *37*
30:19    *129*
31:6    *78*

**Joshua**
24:15    *110*

**1 Kings**
3:5-13    *147*

**2 Chronicles**
32:31    *30*

**Job**
1:1–2:8    *119*
1:1–2:11    *94*
3–31    *94*
5:7    *9*
10:8-12    *129*
13:15    *57*
13:16    *75*
23:10    *13, 25*
28:12-20, 23-24,
    28    *147*
31:15    *129*
42:1-6    *30*
42:2-6    *136–37*

**Psalms**
16:8-11    *52*
22:11    *11*
23:4    *145*
34:17, 19    *76*
37:39-40    *76*
51:12    *67*
66:10    *121*
91:3    *76*
97:10    *76*
100:3    *129*

119:11   *57*
139:13-16   *129*

**Proverbs**
2:2-7   *148*
3:5-7   *148*
4:11   *148*
8:12   *148*
10:8   *148*
14:8   *148*
22:11   *55*
29:25   *106*

**Ecclesiastes**
2:17   *11*

**Isaiah**
26:3-4   *111*
40:1   *145*
40:28-31   *84*
43:1-3   *81*
43:2   *57*
45:7   *25*
49:13   *145*
51:3   *145*
53:7, 9   *96*
53   *38, 98*
55:9   *23*
61:2   *145*

**Jeremiah**
29:11   *47*
29:11-13   *148*

**Daniel**
1:8   *53*
1:8-16   *55*
2:31-35, 38   *55*
2:48-49   *56*
3:1, 6   *55*
3:12, 17-18   *56*
3:24-25   *57*
3:28   *58*
6:3   *59*
6:5   *59–60*
6:10   *60*
6:16   *61*
6:17-23   *62*

**Matthew**
4:1-11   *118*
5:4   *145*
5:10-12   *17*
5:11-12   *122*
5:12   *139*
5:13-14   *19*
6:19-21   *88*
6:24   *33*
6:30-34   *109*
7:7-11   *148*
7:24-27   *104, 110*
10:18-20   *9*
10:21-25   *93*
10:24   *105*
10:25   *106*
10:29-31   *108*
10:34-37   *110*
10:38-39   *111*

12:34-37    *96*
15:18-19    *96*
16:24-25    *75*
18:6, 14    *129*
20:20-23    *143*
22:36-37    *37*
25:31    *124*
26:57-63    *97*

**Mark**
1:21-27    *118*
5:1-20    *118*
8:38    *77*
10:17-22    *33*
13:9-13    *17*
14:33    *11*
15:3-5    *97*

**Luke**
4:25-30    *20*
6:22-23    *124*
6:40    *105*
11:13    *77*
14:26    *37*
17:30    *124*
22:31-32    *39*
23:9    *97*
23:46    *98*

**John**
9:2-3    *94*
10:27-28    *77*
11:33    *11*
12:31    *18*

14:26-27    *51*
14:27    *108, 114*
14:30    *18*
14–16    *77*
15:1-2    *40*
15:5    *99*
15:18-21    *92–93*
15:18-19    *16*
15:20    *20*
15:21    *20–21*
15–16    *121*
16:20-22    *139*
16:33    *11, 22, 114*
17:9-19    *40*
19:9    *97*

**Acts**
1:8    *77*
2:24-25    *51*
4:17-21    *60*
5:40-41    *124*
5:41    *20*
6:5    *46, 49*
6:8    *47*
6:8-10    *46*
6:11-15    *48*
6:15    *47–48*
6–7    *45, 125*
7:55-56    *51*
7:55    *49*
7:57-60    *46*
7:60    *47*
8:1    *45*
9:16    *67*

9:31 *145*
13:50-51 *66*
14:5-7, 19-21 *66*
14:19-20 *80*
16:19-24 *66*
16:22-33 *71*
17:22-23 *21*
20:18-35 *66*
20:24 *69*
20:29-32 *59*
21:13 *67*
21:27 *66*
23:3-5 *97*
26:16 *77*
28:17 *66*
28:30-31 *69*

**Romans**
1:10 *68*
1:14-15 *66*
1:15 *69*
1:18–2:2 *21*
8:6 *115*
8:9 *125*
8:15-17 *78*
8:18-24 *34–35*
8:18 *85*
8:26 *77*
8:28-39 *74*
8:28 *25, 75, 77, 116, 122, 135*
8:32 *146*
12:1-2 *58, 110*
12:1 *132*

12:3 *31*
12:17-21 *99*
13:1-7 *128*
15:19 *66*
15:30 *76*

**1 Corinthians**
1:20 *43*
1:21-25 *22*
3:9-15 *143*
4:16 *66*
9:16 *69*
9:24-25 *89*
10:13 *122*
11:1 *66*
12:26 *146*

**2 Corinthians**
1:3-8 *144*
1:4 *39, 145*
1:5 *145*
1:6-7 *146*
2:2 *92*
3:7-11 *49*
4:1 *81*
4:5 *79*
4:7-18 *20*
4:7 *79–80*
4:8-9 *11, 79*
4:11-15 *145*
4:16-18 *35, 82*
4:16 *83*
4:17 *85*
4:18 *87*

5:1-8    *35–36*
5:7    *150*
5:10    *143*
10:3-5    *118*
11:14    *18*
11:23-27    *66, 145*
11:23-31    *52*
12:7    *31*
12:7-10    *111*
12:9-10    *32*
12:9    *47*
12:10    *67*
12:15    *66*
13:5    *106*

## Galatians
1:6    *66*
1:15    *129*
2:20    *20*
3:6-7    *29*
4:14-20    *66*
5:22    *67*
6:17    *67, 124*

## Ephesians
1:11-14    *149*
1:11-13    *139*
2:14-15    *114*
3:1    *70*
3:16    *84*
4:24    *84*
5:18    *50–51*
6:10-18    *40*

6:15    *115*
6:19    *76*

## Philippians
1:7    *68*
1:8    *145*
1:12-20    *59*
1:13    *71*
1:15, 17    *73*
1:18    *74*
1:19    *77*
1:19-21    *75*
1:20    *66*
1:21    *78*
1:29-30    *124*
2:8-9    *38, 86*
2:15    *19*
2:17    *67*
3:1-16    *66*
3:7-14    *74*
3:7-11    *12*
3:8    *66*
3:10    *20, 124*
3:14-17    *107*
3:17    *66*
4:4    *67*
4:6-7    *113*
4:6    *112*
4:7    *114*
4:9    *114*
4:11-13    *111*
4:11    *116*
4:13    *51*

4:18    *67*
4:22    *71*

**Colossians**
1:24    *124*
2:10-12    *20*
3:1-2    *36, 51*
3:2, 10    *84*
3:15    *114*
3:16    *105*
4:10, 18    *70*

**1 Thessalonians**
2:1-12    *66*
2:7    *145*
4:11    *128*
5:16    *67*
5:23    *114*

**2 Thessalonians**
1:4-7    *131*
3:11    *128*

**1 Timothy**
5:13    *128*

**2 Timothy**
1:7-8    *107*
1:15    *73*
2:8    *100*
2:12    *142*
3:12    *9, 22, 95, 121*
4:10    *66–67*
4:16    *66–67, 73*
4:17    *67*

**Titus**
3:1-4    *128*

**Philemon**
1, 9    *70*

**Hebrews**
1:1-2    *100*
2:10    *93*
2:18    *39*
4:14-16    *100*
4:15    *39*
5:7-9    *37–38*
5:8-9    *93*
5:8    *38*
11:1, 3, 6    *87*
11:13-16    *150*
11:17-19    *29*
11:24-26    *34*
12:1-2    *44, 63, 80*
12:2    *98, 100*
12:3    *80*
12:5-13    *131*
13:5-6    *51*
13:8    *78*

**James**
1:2-4    *40, 141–42*
1:5    *148*
1:9-10    *149*
1:25-27    *25*
2:14-17    *25*
4:4    *22*
4:6    *47*

4:7     *117*
4:14    *85*
5:16    *76*

**1 Peter**
1:3-6     *149*
1:3-7     *138*
1:4     *138–39*
1:6-7     *86*
1:7     *141*
2:11-19     *128*
2:20-23     *92, 95*
2:20     *47*
2:21     *93, 95*
2:22-23     *96*
2:23     *96–98*
3:14     *47*
3:15     *71*
4:7     *130*
4:12     *22, 121, 122*
4:12-14     *120–21*
4:13-14     *125*
4:13     *76, 86, 122, 124*
4:14     *47, 48, 51, 124*
4:15     *128*
4:15-19     *127*
4:17-19     *131*
4:17     *130*
5:6-10     *99*
5:6-7     *111*
5:8-9     *117*
5:10     *84, 113, 142*

**1 John**
2:6     *105*
2:15     *22*
3:12     *19*
3:13     *121*
4:4     *117*

**2 John**
8     *143*

**Revelation**
2:10     *144*
4-5     *142*
20:1-3     *118*

# SUBJECT INDEX

**A**

Abel   *19*

Abraham

    test of faith (Gen. 22)   *26, 28, 29*

    test of first love (Gen. 22)   *36*

Antiabortion (pro-life) activity   *129*

Apostle Paul   *19, 20, 45*

    his background   *65*

    on comfort   *144*

    commitment to the Gospel   *69, 74*

    concerning Abraham   *28*

    concerning death   *75*

    concerning fullness of Spirit   *49*

    concerning self-sacrifice   *58*

    concerning "things above"   *51*

    confidence in Christ's promises   *77*

    confidence in God's Word   *75*

    confidence in prayer   *76*

    confidence as a role model   *66*

    confidence in Spirit   *77*

    counsel to Timothy   *100*

    his detractors   *59, 72*

    eternal hope   *34–35*

    on fear   *106*

    illustration of clay pot   *79*

    instance as poor example   *97*

    joy in spite of suffering   *68*

    and "messenger of Satan"   *31*

    ministry to Roman guards   *71*

and paradoxes of suffering    *78*
preaching in Athens    *21*
prisoner in Philippi    *70*
prisoner in Rome    *68*
regarding comfort to others    *39*
extra revelations    *31*
on rewards    *142*
on spiritual warfare    *118*
his sufferings    *11*
warning of persecution    *9*
world's wisdom    *22*
Apostle Peter    *45, 48, 51, 60*
on entrusting    *131*
regarding Holy Spirit    *124*
on joy in suffering    *122*
on judgment of believers    *130*
on persecution    *121*
perspectives on salvation    *139*
quote of Septuagint    *96*
on Satan    *118*
on suffering    *93*
on "troublesome meddler"    *128*
Application, of Scripture    *119*
Assurance of salvation    *138*
Athletes (professional)    *30*
Attitude
toward suffering (1 Peter 4:12-14)    *120*
toward suffering (1 Peter 4:15-19)    *127*
usage of word (slang)    *120*

### B

Babylon    *52*
Bonar, Horatius    *135*
Branch Davidian incident    *17*

Bull, Geoffrey    *133*

## C
Cain    *19*
Chaldea, Chaldean. See Babylon
Chesterton, G.K.    *26*
"Christian bashing"    *9*
Comfort, as lesson from suffering    *144*
Cowper, William    *151*
Cranmer, Archbishop Thomas (martyr)    *125*

## D
Daniel    *12, 52*
    convictions of    *53–54, 60–61*
    deportation of    *54*
    in lions' den    *58*
    as mentor    *58*
    opponents of    *60*
Daniel, Book of    *52*
Daniel, friends of    *12, 52*
    convictions of    *54, 58*
    as exiles    *54*
    and fiery furnace    *53*
Darius    *60*
Detractors
    from within church    *72*
    at Corinth    *78*
    defined    *72*
    of Paul. See also Apostle Paul    *73, 78*
Diet of Worms    *8*
Discipleship    *13*
    Jesus sets standard    *106*
    and reaction to the unexpected    *109–13*
    relationship to suffering    *105*

**E**

Empathy, lesson of  *38*
Endurance (in suffering)  *81*
    importance of the eternal  *87*
    because future takes priority  *85*
    because of spiritual's preeminence  *83*
    modern aversion to  *82*
    reasons for  *82*


**F**

Faith
    essence of  *87*
    genuineness of  *141*
Fear  *106*
Feinberg, C.L.  *113*
First love  *36*


**G**

Gehrig, Lou  *31*
Glory, future  *88, 143*
    defined  *84, 86*
    in 2 Corinthians 4:16-18  *82*
    in 1 Peter 1:6-7  *86*
"God Moves in a Mysterious Way" (hymn)  *151*
God's blessings, lesson of  *37*
God's sovereignty  *23*
    and adversity  *24*
    comfort from  *25*
Gold, compared to faith  *141*
Government, believer's role in  *128*
Grace in suffering (defined)  *47*

**H**

Holy Spirit
    fullness of (defined)   *49*
    glory of   *125*
    resting upon believers   *124*
    Stephen filled with   *49*
Hope, eternal   *23, 34, 41*
Humility   *30*
    as lesson from suffering   *148*
    and Paul   *31*


**I**

Inheritance, eternal (protected)   *138*
Isaac   *26-29, 36*


**J**

James and John (positions in kingdom)   *143*
Jansen, Dan   *107*
Jesus Christ
    appearance in Daniel   *57*
    best role model   *100*
    common perceptions   *91*
    compared to sheep (silence)   *97*
    concerning true joy   *139*
    entrusted Himself to God   *98*
    example of obedience   *37–38*
    followers will be hated   *20*
    hated by religious system   *19–20*
    as High Priest   *39*
    on the kingdom of God   *143*
    preached by Stephen   *45–46*
    predicts hostility (Upper Room)   *16*
    predicts hostility from world   *92*
    on putting Him first   *37*

regarding persecution  *9, 11*

regarding persecution (Sermon on Mount)  *16–17*

and 2 Peter 2:21  *95*

seen by Stephen  *51*

sinless sufferer  *94*

as Suffering Servant  *38, 96–98*

as the suffering One  *94*

warning on materialism  *33*

Job

lessons from his suffering  *136*

and purpose of God  *113*

and wisdom  *147*

Joy

fruit of Spirit  *67*

as lesson of suffering  *137*

at Resurrection  *139*

true nature of  *138*


**L**

Latimer, Bishop Hugh (martyr)  *99*

Lenski, R.C.H.  *150*

Lincoln, Abraham  *72*

Lloyd-Jones, D. Martyn  *122–23*

Lockyer, Herbert  *66*

Lou Gehrig's disease  *31, 74*

Luther, Martin

at Diet of Worms  *8*

faithfulness to truth  *7*

reaction to crisis  *9*


**M**

Martyrdom

recent statistics  *10*

threat of   *9*

Materialism
    as lesson from suffering   *32*
    Moses' example toward   *34*
    as part of society   *33*
Moses, compared to Stephen   *45*


**N**

Natural disasters   *149*
    beyond man's control   *103*
    in Jesus' parable   *104*
Nebuchadnezzar   *54*
    dream of statue   *55*
    glorifies God   *58*


**O**

Orange County (bankruptcy)   *109*


**P**

Partnership in suffering   *147*
Peace (of God), definition   *113–14*
Persecution. See also Apostle Paul; Apostle; Jesus Christ
    from unbelieving family   *110*
    to be expected   *11, 105*
Persian Gulf War   *39–40*
Philippian believers   *68, 73*
Philippians, letter to   *68–69*
Pink, A.W.   *23*
Polycarp (martyr)   *60–61*
Prayer, and gratefulness   *112*
Preventive spiritual maintenence   *111*
Providence (of God)
    compared to miracle   *115*

definition of    *114–15*

and Joseph    *116*


**R**

Reformation (Protestant)    *7*

Role models. See also Apostle Paul; Jesus Christ    *12*

    celebrities as    *43*

    in Scripture    *44*


**S**

Satan

    as "angel of light"    *18*

    author of world system    *18, 22*

    binding of    *117–18*

    "messenger of"    *31–32*

    and Paul    *31*

    and Peter    *39*

    role in suffering    *118*

    and world    *10*

Servant (as disciple)    *105*

    free from fear    *106*

    is prepared    *109*

    not exempt from persecution    *105*

Sin

    as cause for suffering    *94*

    and the mouth    *96*

Sovereignty of God    *12*

    definition of    *23–24*

    role in adversity    *15–16*

Spiritual warfare    *117*

Stephen    *12*

    comparison to Moses    *48*

    grace in suffering    *46*

    his death    *47–52*

his strategic place    *45*
his trust in God    *47–48*
looked to Christ    *51*
ministry in Acts    *45–46*
serenity in suffering    *47*
Spirit-filled    *49*
Strength, lesson of    *39*

## W

"What'er My God Ordains Is Right" (hymn)    *16*
Wisdom
definition of    *148*
and James    *148*
and Job    *147*
and Solomon    *147*
Woodbridge, John    *44*
World Trade Center bombing    *17*